Not by Food Alone

Recipes and Tales from the Shabbat Table at Shanti House

KOSHER

ShantiHouse
A Warm Home for Youth At Risk

Not by Food Alone

Recipes and Tales from the Shabbat Table at Shanti House

KOSHER

Editor: Michal Moses

English editor: Shoshana Brickman

Graphic editor and design: Ayelet Yehuda
English Layout: A.N. Computer Services
Photograph editors: Yasmin & Arye Photographers
Producers: Michal Moses, Dana Livnat-Gazit
Production assistants: Shaili Talker and Shlomit Flesh
Story collection and selection: Michael ben Yosef
Linguistic editor: Marilyn Moses

Photographers: Ilit Azolay, Shachar Fleischmann, Kfir Harbi, Eran Lam, Gilad Larom, Daniel Layla, Michal Lenart, Philip Metrai, Yossi Salis, Adi Shiovits, Doron Gafni, Danya Weiner, Danny Yanai, Yasmin & Arye Photographers

Stylists: Chanoch Bar Shalom, Natasha Haimovich, Dariya Karagula, Nurit Kariv

© All rights reserved
Shanti House
17 Simtat Shlush,
P.O. Box 50041
Tel Aviv 61500 Israel

This publication is protected under federal copyright laws. Reproduction or distribution is prohibited unless specifically authorized. This includes, but is not limited to, any form of reproduction or distribution on or through the Internet, scanning, copying, photographing, modifying, or reprinting.

www.shanti.org.il

www.shanti.org.il/eng

Photograph calibration and color separation: ArtScan
Printing: Grapholit Printing Works Incorporated

ISBN 978-965-229-861-4

"…and I don't need to search in the garbage
Or be afraid of police officers at night?"
The angel shakes his head.
'No.' Here, you have all the support."

From the poem "Angel from Heaven"
published in the book, Excuse us for being born, Shanti Children Write about Everything

Dedicated with love

To the children of Shanti House

Contents

Introduction	8
Acknowledgements	10
A special thanks	12
Lighting the Candles	14
Shalom Aleichem	15
Woman of Valor	16
Blessing over the Wine	17
Shabbat Challah Uri Scheft	18
Child of Shabbat	19

Salads

Carrot and Kohlrabi Salad with Citrus Vinaigrette and Walnuts Yair Feinberg	22
Quinoa and Dried Fruit Salad Yair Feinberg	22
The Wheel Goes Round	23
Cooked Olive Salad Aviv Moshe	24
Greek Eggplant Salad Aviv Moshe	24
Roasted Vegetable Salad Aviv Moshe	24
Roasted Hot Pepper Salad Aviv Moshe	25
Cherry Tomato Salad with Scallions Aviv Moshe	25
Mend the World	25
Roasted Eggplant and Pepper Salad, with Tahini Daniel Zach	26
Fresh Herb, Cashew, and Lemon Salad Daniel Zach	26
Listen to a Whisper or Wait for a Rude Awakening	27
Beet Tahini with Chickpea and Black Lentil Salad Ayelet Or	28
Raw Beet Salad Shaoul Ben Aderet	28
Apio: Root Vegetable Dish Kochava Manor	29
Remembering the Good; Forgetting the Bad	29
Chickpea Casserole with Ginger, Tomato, and Date Honey Einav Berman	30
Cauliflower, Pepper, and Citrus Casserole Einav Berman	30
Steamed Basmati Rice Einav Berman	31
Criticism and Dirty Laundry	31

Fish

Asian Chreime on a Bed of Couscous Eyal Lavi	34
A Tale of Two Brothers	35
Noodles and Frika with Slices of Fish, Chimichurri, Tomatoes and Pickled Lemons Golan Gorfinkel	36
The Butterfly	37
Seared Nile Perch in Garlic and Lemon, with Moroccan Salsa Ayelet Or	38
The Mountain	39
Nile Perch with Lemon and Fresh Herbs Shaoul Ben Aderet	40
Coping with Problems	41
Tuscany Baked Fish Avi Bitton	42
On the Side: White Beans with Fresh Herbs	43
A Pair of Socks	43
Nile Perch in Tomato, Pepper, Eggplant and Chickpea Sauce Meir Adoni	44
Swiss Chard Salad Meir Adoni	45
The Fisherman	45
Mafrum Fish in Eggplant, Tomato Sauce and Tahini Chanoch Bar Shalom	46
The Story of the Nails in the Fence	47

Chicken Livers

Liver with Onion Jam Israel Aharoni	50
Chopped Liver Livnat Family	50
The Story of Love	51
Chicken Livers in Turmeric Mariuma	52

Crispy Chicken Liver Salad with Spinach Leaves and Orange Slices Ayelet Or — 52
The Power of Cooperation — 53
Croissants Filled with Chicken Liver Orly Pely Bronstein — 54
A Tale of Two Monks — 55

Chicken

Chicken Quarters Baked in Parchment Paper Chanoch Bar Shalom — 58
Thank you — 59
Maschan Dror Pilz — 60
The Painting — 61
Sunday Shnitzel Razi Livnat — 62
The Man and the Monkey — 63
Tabchah Balkra'ah: Chicken in Pumpkin and Potatoes Zevik Laisten — 64
Chicken with Artichokes Nir Tzuk — 64
Respect — 65
Paella Chicken Leon Alcalai — 66
The Scottish Farmer and Penicillin — 67
Chicken in Apples, Cinnamon and Caramel Sauce Segev Moshe — 68
The Island — 69
Pal'u - Bukharin Rice Dish Ofira Gordon — 70
Bank of Time — 71
Coco: Grandma Ora's Roast Chicken Ora Ben Yosef — 72
The Tools from Hashem (A True Story) — 72
Chicken Stuffed with Ground Meat and Rice Mariuma — 74
Life — 75
Chicken Stuffed with Rice, Mushrooms, and Fresh Herbs Omer Miller — 76
The King Who Had Four Wives — 76
Chicken with Potatoes and Red Peppers Mariuma — 78
Chicken in Coconut Sauce Mariuma — 78
No Price for Love — 79
Chicken Stew with Israeli Couscous and Vegetables Nitzan Raz — 80
The Policy of Monkeys — 81
Citrus Chicken Thighs Israel Aharoni — 82
The Golden Cage — 83
Chicken with Sweet Potatoes, Soy Sauce, and Honey Mariuma — 84
The Large Stones of Life — 84
Chicken Drumsticks Filled with Pickled Lemons, Lentils, and Rice Chanoch Bar Shalom — 86
The Clock — 87
Chicken in Raisins and Olives Rachel Shtark Biniamin — 88
Chicken with String Beans Mariuma — 88
The Tree — 89
Chicken Legs Stuffed with Almonds and Pistachios Chanoch Bar Shalom — 90
White Fava Bean and Olive Oil Spread Chanoch Bar Shalom — 91
The Cracked Bucket — 91

Ground Meat

Stuffed Onions Erez Komarovsky — 94
A Stranger Came to Stay — 94
Braided Puff Pastry with Ground Beef, Eggplant, and Olives Michal Moses — 96
Be Yourself — 97
Meatballs in Lemon Sauce Razi Livnat — 98
Put Down the Glass Today — 99
Vegetables Stuffed with Meat, Rice, and Lentils Daniel Zach — 100
Invitation — 101
Meatballs with Baharat and Hawayij Shaoul Ben Aderet — 102

Contents

Pumpkin in Date Honey and Rosemary Shaoul Ben Aderet ... 102
On The Quality of Hearing ... 103
Meatballs on a Bed of Eggplant and Tomatoes Malca Eliakim ... 104
More Precious Than Diamonds ... 105
Meatlovers Meat Sauce Raphi Aharonovich ... 106
Path of Life ... 106
Meatballs with Peas Mariuma ... 108
Tomatoes Stuffed with Ground Meat and Rice Mariuma ... 108
The Frog's Tale ... 109
Artichokes Filled with Ground Meat Liat Turgeman ... 110
I Ate Lunch With G-d ... 111
Meatballs in Artichoke, Fava Bean, and Sage Casserole Meir Adoni ... 112
Harvard and Stanford ... 113
Meatballs with Eggplant Mariuma ... 114
Only a Smile ... 115
Grape Leaf Cake, with Meat, Rice, Raisins, and Pistachios Zachi Bukshester ... 116
The Farm ... 117
Mafrum Gil Hovav ... 118
Our True Worth ... 119

Desserts
Baked Apples in Crispy Coating Aner Zalel ... 122
A Lesson in Modesty ... 122
Cinnamon Buns Uri Scheft ... 124
The Cookie Bag ... 125
Date Cookies Tzvia Azulai ... 126
Coconut Malabi Tzvia Azulai ... 126
Experience ... 127
Puff Pastry Baklava Ora Ben Yosef ... 128
G-d's Coffee ... 129
Daniel's Chocolate Cake Ben Ami Bertini Shavit ... 130
Semolina Cake Dana Livnat-Gazit ... 131
The Experiment ... 131
Walnut Carrot Cake Micky Shemo ... 132
Quince Jam Yechiel & Ronen Philosoph ... 132
Wine Vinegar ... 133
Raybe Biscuits Hadar Yiftah-Tutya ... 134
Halva Squares Barry Sayag ... 134
A Glass of Milk ... 135
Masapan: Moroccan Marzipan Ayelet Or ... 136
Yoyo: Fried Biscuits Ayelet Or ... 136
The Love Box ... 137

Ingredient Index ... 138
Story Index ... 142
Photographer and Stylist Index ... 143

Introduction

Two pounds of chicken, 2 pounds of rice, 4 pounds of overripe tomatoes that I used to make matbucha (tomato stew). That's how it all started, one Friday night, 31 years ago. There were three pots on the stove, and a great need for me to bestow my guests with a family experience. In some magical way, that small amount of food managed to satisfy everyone–homeless teens, street people, and friends, and I was delighted. From one Shabbat to the next, the magic continued. The tradition of welcoming guests and serving them homemade food worked wonders. Slowly, the human fabric known now as Shanti House was woven.

The Shabbat meal became an important goal in its own right. We never gave up on Kiddush (the blessing over the wine), even during hard times, when we had very few resources. We would walk, the children staying at Shanti House and I, to the Carmel Market and gather food that had been thrown out because it wasn't good enough to sell. From this discarded food, we prepared our Shabbat meal. That's when I understood that if you want to feel the touch of G–d, there is no place for ego or shame. By contrast–it is a right. During difficult moments, we experienced G–d's miracles by receiving freshly baked cakes and freshly caught fish. Food received this way doesn't just satisfy the stomach, but also the soul. It is seasoned with spirituality, and there is no other flavor quite like it.

People who receive the Shabbat with us at Shanti House are, in my eyes, souls that connect with us for a magical moment of family.

Over time, Shanti House became a non-profit organization, and very dear people donated foodstuffs to us for the Shabbat meal: hotels in Tel Aviv, conference halls, and several other contributors, many of whom never knew the angelic role they had in feeding so many hungry children. Every Friday, when all the children and guests gather around the Shabbat table, I like to remind everyone that nothing should be taken for granted in life, and that we must say thanks every day for what we have.

In 2005, Michael joined the Shanti family. His connection and contribution to the existence of Shanti House was expressed, among other things, in the Shabbat meals. Every week, after I had summarized the week that had passed with the children, we make Kiddush and then it is Michael's turn to tell a short story with a moral. Through his stories, Michael often succeeds in moving the young souls, while at the same time, teaching a lesson, an educational message that gives them strength, wisdom, and desire to be people who are better. The children at Shanti House look forward to these stories eagerly.

The idea to collect Michael's stories with my recipes for Shabbat had already been raised in 2007. The moment arrived in December 2008, when a charming woman–Michal Moses–entered our lives. It was her idea to prepare a book of recipes for Shabbat. I told her about my idea, and it clicked. She immediately took it upon herself, with the assistance of dear Dana Livnat-Gazit. These two women enlisted 32 chefs, along with food photographers, stylists, Shanti House volunteers, and myself, all of us working as volunteers, and this cookbook was born.

This book brings the scents, voices, colors, and tastes of our Shabbat meal at Shanti House. The recipes are spread out on 108 pages, two pages for every one of the 54 Shabbats in every year. Every Shabbat is accompanied by a recipe or two, and a story selected from the stories that Michael traditionally tells after Kiddush.

As for the recipes, these consist of the simplest possible ingredients, those which are found in the Shanti House pantry: frozen fish filets, chicken livers, ground meat, and chicken pieces. The book is kosher, thus all of the dishes are either meat-based or pareve.

Dear parents,
I hope that you learn to understand the intense power of the Shabbat meal, to unite family members and support them. Weekends strengthen and prepare all of us for the challenges that each new week brings. There is no doubt in my heart that, thanks to that Shabbat evening 31 years ago, and thanks to the many Shabbat meals that we have held since then, Shanti House was created, and continues to exist.

Wishing you a hearty appetite,
And with love,
Mariuma
And the Entire Shanti House Family

Acknowledgements

Now that we have finished collecting the recipes and stories, and our souls are satiated with cooked dishes, the time has come to write our thanks. We start by counting individual people, but as we write, we remember more and more names. The list gets longer, and our hearts widen with the increase of volunteers that contributed to this book. We met many wonderful people along the way, and this page is dedicated, with love, to them all.

First of all, to the chef and food journalist Michal Moses, and to Dana Livnat-Gazit, for the desire, achievement, and passion that they discovered in the implementation of this special project. It is only thanks to their intensity and depth that this book was created.

For the contribution of leading chefs, volunteers who cook at Shanti House on a regular basis, photographers, stylists, lawyer, public relations people, and the staff at Shanti House. For convenience, we'll list these names in alphabetical order:

To the chefs, who created delicacies from the simplest possible ingredients: Meir Adoni, Israel Aharoni, Raphi Aharonovich, Leon Alcalai, Tzvia Azulai, Chanoch Bar Shalom, Shaoul Ben Aderet, Einav Berman, Avi Bitton, Orly Pely Bronstein, Zachi Bukshester, Yair Feinberg, Golan Gorfinkel, Gil Hovav, Erez Komarovsky, Eyal Lavi, Omer Miller, Michal Moses, Aviv Moshe, Segev Moshe, Ayelet Or, Yechiel & Ronen Philosoph, Dror Pilz, Nitzan Raz, Barry Sayag, Uri Scheft, Ben Ami Bertini Shavit, Micky Shemo, Nir Tzuk, Hadar Yiftah-Tutya, Daniel Zach, Aner Zalel.

To the volunteers, who cook with devotion and love at Shanti House on a regular basis: Ora Ben Yosef, Malca Elyakim, Ofira Gordon, Zevik Laisten, Razi Livnat, Dana Livnat-Gazit, Rachel Shtark Biniamin, Liat Turgeman.

To the photographers, who helped make this book an album as well as a cookbook: Ilit Azolay, Shachar Fleischmann, Doron Gafni, Kfir Harbi, Eran Lam, Daniel Layla, Gilad Larom, Philippe Matrai, Yosi Salis, Adi Shiovits, Danya Weiner, Danny Yanai.

To the stylists, who met the not-so-simple challenge of photographing in the Shanti House using authentic serving dishes and accessories from the Shanti House: Natasha Haimovich, Dariya Karagula, Nurit Kariv.

To the editor of the Hebrew version, Michal Moses, and the English version, Shoshana Brickman.

To the Hebrew proofreader Matat Eshet, and to those who helped with the proofreading: Avner & Osnat Hacohen.

To the English translators, Irit Baher, Josanne Ben Chur, Shoshana Brickman, Marilyn Moses, and Lilly Vered, who worked as a team to translate these recipes and stories.

To Orly Pely Bronstein who contributed her experience in editing recipes

To dear Mrs. Miriam Mimi Nofech Mozes, to Dov Eichenwald and Zvika Meir, from "Yediyot Sefarime," on their assistance distributing this book to bookstores.

To Hacohen & Co Law Office, and especially to attorney Irit Hacohen, for her assistance and legal advice. To Ofer Gazit & Zohar Livnat, for their personal and special help.

To the public relations staff: Yuval Katz, Orit Levy, Eran Levy-Katz from Guy Tatsa PR Office.

To Shlomit Flesh and Shaili Talker from Shanti House, who helped co-produce the book.

To Sari Perl, who helped crystallize the concept at the beginning of the way.

To all Shanti House supporters.

To Leny Ehrman, of the Shanti House organization, who encouraged me at every moment to bring this project to fruition, and helped us come up with the name of the book.

Very special thanks to Raya Strauss and to Doron & Marianne Livnat, for their support over long years, and their never-ending belief in this, my life's project.

Thank You!
Shanti House Family

A Special Thanks to the Strauss Group

I still vividly remember the first time a Strauss truck unpacked boxes of the company's products-contributions to the Shanti. The children devoured the products, especially the desserts. Each child ate four Milky at least, one right after the other! Later, there was the excitement of Strauss hummus. That still hasn't been forgotten, and remains a permanent fixture on our Shabbat table.

The same truck that first came to us more than ten years ago continues to stop at Shanti House every week. In retrospect, that visit can be viewed as the beginning of a remarkable relationship. Even though Strauss was a big company even then, the relationship with Shanti House was then, as today, intimate, personal, like a family, really.

After collecting the material for this book, we realized that we needed a final push to get the book finished. We turned to the people we knew, and to those who know us, those who really care. When the people at Strauss saw the sketches for the book, the excitement was enormous. The Strauss group and its people have been personal guides for many years, and that's the most impressive thing of all. There is no limit to the gratitude felt by the Shanti House family towards Strauss, for its authentic assistance in realizing this book, and in general.

Lighting the Candles

On Friday evening, the woman of the house lights the candles and makes the following blessing:

Blessed are You, Lord our G-d, King of the Universe, Who sanctified us with His commandments, and commanded us to light the holy Shabbat light.

There are some people who add the following:
May it be Your will, Hashem, my G-d and the G-d of my forefathers, that You show favor to me
(my husband, my sons, my daughters, my father, my mother)
and all my relatives, and that You grant us and all Israel a good and long life.
That You remember us with a beneficent memory and blessing.
That You consider us with a consideration of salvation and compassion.
That You bless us with great blessings. That You make our households complete.
That You cause Your Presence to dwell among us.
Grant me the privilege me to raise children and grandchildren who are wise and understanding,
who love Hashem and fear G-d, people of truth, holy offspring, attached to Hashem,
who illuminate the world with Torah and good deeds and with every labor in the service of the Creator.
Please, hear my supplication at this time, in the merit of Sarah, Rivkah, Rachel, and Leah,
our mothers, and cause our light to illuminate, so that it is never extinguished,
and let Your countenance shine so that we are saved. Amen.

בערב השבת תדליק האישה את הנרות ותברך:
ברוך אתה ה', אלהינו מלך העולם, אשר קדשנו במצותיו, וציונו להדליק נר של שבת.

יש הנוהגות להוסיף:
יהי רצון מלפניך ה' אלהי ואלהי אבותי שתחונן אותי (ואת אישי ואת בני ואת בנותי ואת אבי ואת אמי) ואת כל קרובי, ותתן לנו ולכל ישראל חיים טובים וארוכים, ותזכרנו בזכרון טובה וברכה, ותפקדנו בפקודת ישועה ורחמים, ותברכנו ברכות גדולות, ותשלים בתינו, ותשכן שכינתך בינינו, וזכני לגדל בנים ובני בנים חכמים ונבונים, אוהבי ה' יראי אלהים אנשי אמת, זרע קדש בה' דבקים, ומאירים את העולם בתורה ומעשים טובים ובכל מלאכת עבודת הבורא. אנא שמע את תחינתי בעת הזאת בזכות שרה ורבקה ורחל ולאה אמותנו, והאר נרנו שלא יכבה לעולם ועד, והאר פניך ונשעה, אמן.

Shalom Aleichem

Songs for Shabbat
In many homes, songs are sung after the candles have been lit, to welcome the Shabbat, and draw the family together.

Shalom Aleichem
Peace upon you, ministering angels, angels of the Exalted One-from the King Who reigns over kings, the Holy One, blessed is He. Three times.

Come for peace, angels of peace, angels of the Exalted One-from the King Who reigns over kings, the Holy One, Blessed is He. Three times.

Bless me for peace, angels of peace, angels of the Exalted One-from the King Who reigns over kings, the Holy One, Blessed is He. Three times.

Depart in peace, angels of peace, angels of the Exalted One-from the King who reigns over kings, the Holy One, Blessed is He. Three times.

זמירות קודם הקידוש והסעודה:

שלום עליכם מלאכי השרת מלאכי עליון
ממלך מלכי המלכים הקדוש ברוך הוא שלוש פעמים

בואכם לשלום מלאכי השרת מלאכי עליון
ממלך מלכי המלכים הקדוש ברוך הוא שלוש פעמים

ברכוני לשלום מלאכי השרת מלאכי עליון
ממלך מלכי המלכים הקדוש ברוך הוא שלוש פעמים

צאתכם לשלום מלאכי השרת מלאכי עליון
ממלך מלכי המלכים הקדוש ברוך הוא שלוש פעמים

כי מלאכיו יצוה לך לשמרך בכל דרכך:
יהוה ישמר צאתך ובואך מעתה ועד עולם

Woman of Valor

This song is sung in praise of the woman of the house, for all that she has done for her household during the week.

An accomplished woman, who can find?
Her value is far beyond pearls.
Her husband's heart relies on her,
and he shall lack no fortune.
She does him good and not evil,
all the days of her life.
She seeks wool and linen,
and her hands work willingly.
She is like the merchant's ships,
she brings food from afar.
She wakes while it is still night,
and feeds her household, and gives a portion to her maids.
She plans for a field, and buys it; with the fruit of her handiwork she plants a vineyard.
She girds her loins in strength,
and makes her arms strong.
She knows that her merchandise is good;
her candle does not go out at night.
She sets her hands to the distaff,
and holds the spindle in her hands.
She extends her hands to the poor,
and reaches out to the needy.
She does not fear for her household because of snow,
because her whole household is warmly dressed.
She makes covers for herself,
her clothing is fine linen and purple.
Her husband is well known at the gates,
where he sits with the elders of the land.
She makes a garment and sells it,
and she delivers aprons to the peddler.
Strength and honor are her clothing,
she smiles at her future.
She opens her mouth in wisdom,
and the lesson of kindness is on her tongue.
She anticipates the needs of her household,
and does not eat the bread of idleness.
Her children rise and praise her,
her husband celebrates her too.
Many women have achieved valor,
but you surpass them all.
Charm is deceptive, and beauty is vain,
but a woman who fears G-d, she shall be praised.
Give her of the fruit of her hands,
and she will be praised at the gates for her works.

אשת חיל

אשת חיל מי ימצא, ורחוק מפנינים מִכְרָהּ.
בטח בה לב בעלה ושלל לא יחסר.
גמלתהו טוב ולא רע, כל ימי חייה.
דרשה צמר ופשתים, ותעש בחפץ כפיה.
היתה כאניות סוחר, ממרחק תביא לחמה.
ותקם בעוד לילה, ותתן טרף לביתה וחוק לנערותיה.
זממה שדה ותקחהו, מפרי כפיה נטעה כרם.
חגרה בעוז מתניה, ותאמץ זרועותיה.
טעמה כי טוב סחרה, לא יכבה בלילה נרה.
ידיה שלחה בכישור, וכפיה תמכו פלך.
כפה פרשה לעני, וידיה שלחה לאביון.
לא תירא לביתה משלג, כי כל ביתה לבוש שנים.
מרבדים עשתה לה, שש וארגמן לבושה.
נודע בשערים בעלה בשבתו עם זקני ארץ.
סדין עשתה ותמכור, וחגור נתנה לכנעני.
עוז והדר לבושה, ותשחק ליום אחרון.
פיה פתחה בחכמה, ותורת חסד על לשונה.
צופיה הליכות ביתה, ולחם עצלות לא תאכל.
קמו בניה ויאשרוה, בעלה ויהללה.
רבות בנות עשו חיל, ואת עלית על כולנה.
שקר החן והבל היופי, אשה יראת ה' היא תתהלל.
תנו לה מפרי ידיה, ויהללוה בשערים מעשיה.

Shabbat Dinner

Blessing over the Wine
The head of the household stands at the head of the table, raises a cup of wine, and recites the following blessing:

The sixth day: And the heavens and earth, and all their array, were finished.
And G-d finished by the seventh day His work which He had done, and He rested on the seventh day from all His work which He had done: And G-d blessed the seventh day and made it holy. Because He rested on it from all His work, which G-d had created to make.
Attention, gentlemen! Blessed are You, Hashem, our G-d, King of the universe, Who creates the fruit of the vine.
Blessed are You, Lord our G-d, King of the world, Who made us holy with His commandments, and favored us, and gave us His holy Shabbat as a heritage, as a reminder of Creation. For that day is first of the holy festivals, a memorial of the exodus from Egypt.
For You chose us, and sanctified us, from all the nations. And gave us Your holy Shabbat with love and goodwill, as a heritage. Blessed are You, Lord, Who sanctifies the Shabbat. Amen.

The person holding the wine glass takes the first sip of wine, then distributes the wine among all the people at the table.

Ritual Hand Washing
Everyone rises from the table, washes their hands, and says the following blessing:

Blessed are You, Lord our G-d, King of the Universe, Who sanctified us with His commandments, and commanded us on the washing of the hands.

Blessing over the Challah
After the ritual hand washing, everyone returns to the table, and the following blessing is made on two challahs:
Blessed are You, Lord our G-d, King of the Universe, Who brings forth bread from the earth.

The challah is then ripped by hand and distributed among all the people at the table.

The Sabbath Meal Begins

יום השישי: ויכלו השמים והארץ וכל צבאם: ויכל אלהים ביום השביעי מלאכתו אשר עשה. וישבות ביום השביעי מכל מלאכתו אשר עשה: ויברך אלהים את יום השביעי ויקדש אותו. כי בו שבת מכל מלאכתו אשר ברא אלהים לעשות:
סברי מרנן ועונים לחיים

ברוך אתה ה', אלהינו מלך העולם,
בורא פרי הגפן ועונים אמן.

ברוך אתה ה', אלהינו מלך העולם, אשר קדשנו במצותיו ורצה בנו, ושבת קדשו באהבה וברצון הנחילנו, זכרון למעשה בראשית, תחילה למקרא קדש, זכר ליציאת מצרים. ושבת קדשך באהבה וברצון הנחלתנו: ברוך אתה ה', מקדש השבת:

יטעם מהכוס ויחלק לכל המסובין. ייטול ידיו ויברך:
ברוך אתה ה', אלהינו מלך העולם,
אשר קדשנו במצותיו וציונו על נטילת ידים:

יברך על שתי החלות:
ברוך אתה ה', אלהינו מלך העולם,
המוציא לחם מן הארץ:
יבצע החלה ויטעם, יחלק לכל המסובין (לפחות כזית לכל אחד)

סעודת השבת

17

Shabbat Challah
Uri Scheft, Lehamim Bakery

Shabbat simply isn't complete without challah, the beloved egg bread that fragrantly marks the end of the week.
Makes 2 large challahs and 12 round buns

Dough
1⅔ cups (400 ml) water
One 1½ ounce (50 gram) cube fresh yeast
8 cups (1 kilogram) white flour, plus more for dusting
2 large eggs
½ cup + 1 tablespoon (120 grams) sugar
2 teaspoons (15 grams) salt
⅓ cup (80 ml) oil

Topping
1 egg, beaten
2 to 3 teaspoons water
Salt
Handful sesame seeds, poppy seeds, or other seeds

Prepare dough: Pour water in the bowl of an electric mixer. Add yeast and mix until yeast dissolves. Add flour and eggs and knead with the dough hook over low speed for about 30 seconds. Add sugar, salt, and oil, and knead for another 3 minutes. Increase speed to medium and knead for 4 minutes, until texture is smooth. Turn out dough onto a lightly floured surface, and knead until elastic, flexible and not too soft. Shape into a ball, place in a lightly floured bowl, and cover with a clean kitchen towel. Set aside to rise for about 40 minutes.

Turn out dough, shape into a flattened rectangle, and divide into 3 even pieces. You'll use one piece to make a dozen small buns, and the other pieces to make braided challahs.

To make braided challah, divide dough into 3 even pieces. Roll each piece into a sausage, then press sausages together at one end. Plait them into a braid, then press the other ends together. To make a round braided challah, connect the two ends of the braided challah to form a ring.

Line a baking sheet with parchment paper, lay challahs on top, and cover with a clean kitchen towel. Set aside to rise for 30 to 40 minutes, until challahs rise but maintain their shape.

To make buns, divide dough into 12 even pieces, and roll each piece into a ball. Line baking sheet with parchment paper, and arrange balls on top. Cover with a clean kitchen towel, and set aside for about 20 minutes, until buns rise but maintain their shape. (These will rise in less time than it takes for the challah to rise.) Preheat oven to 350°F (180°C).

Prepare topping: In a small bowl, combine egg, water, and salt to make egg wash. Just before baking, brush challah tops with egg wash, then sprinkle with seeds. Bake large challahs for about 25 minutes, and challah buns for about 14 minutes, or until challahs are golden on top.

בראשית

Child of Shabbat

I have stuttered since I was four years old. When I was small, my stutter was so bad that sometimes I couldn't even talk. At the same time, I was brave, surrounded by friends, an excellent athlete, and not a bad student-in short, a fairly happy boy. However, every time someone wanted to hurt me, they would refer to my stutter. And it always worked. Always.

One day, when I was six years old, I came home crying. I didn't want to talk to anyone. My father came into my room and asked me what had happened. I wouldn't answer. He kept on asking, and eventually I told him that I hated G‑d…. In the morning, he woke me up and told me the following story:

High in the sky is a huge factory where children are made. The angels there work non-stop, 24 hours a day, preparing children for the entire world. They work under intense pressure, since there is a lot of work, little time, and everything has to be perfect.

There are recipes for all kinds of different children. They have raw material for brains, beauty, and height, for good qualities and bad ones. The angels work very hard, from morning to night. On Fridays, however, just before lunchtime, a bell starts to ring very softly. The angels stop the machines, switch off the factory lights, and go home to prepare for the Shabbat.

Just before the Shabbat meal, the angels put on their festive wings and halos. G‑d himself prepares the meal, which is full of wonderful food. The angels tell stories, sing, and dance. After the meal they go to sleep; everyone is tired from their week of hard work. The only one who isn't tired is G‑d, but he doesn't work on the Shabbat either.

In fact, G‑d is sometimes a bit bored on Shabbat, so sometimes, he creeps into the baby factory and prepares a baby with his own hands. Of course, when G‑d does something, he does it the best way possible, without any instructions or plans, but with all his heart. He uses more raw material for brains, character, and beauty. He adds so many good qualities that sometimes he realizes the child he made was too perfect. He knows that he can't send such a perfect child to earth, because everyone will know G‑d made him.

In order to conceal his involvement, G‑d gives the child a very slight flaw, something unimportant. In one child, he makes a limp; in another, he makes crossed eyes; in another, he creates a stutter. These children are called Children of Shabbat, and you are one of them. So the next time you see a child who limps, has crossed eyes, or stutters a bit, don't laugh at him. He is probably a Child of Shabbat, just like you.

Salads

Salads

Carrot and Kohlrabi Salad with Citrus Vinaigrette and Walnuts
Yair Feinberg, Fein Cuisine

This salad is crispy and fresh, healthy and full of flavor. It looks fantastic as well.
Serves 10

Dressing
2 cups (480 ml) orange juice
2 teaspoons honey
¼ cup (60 ml) freshly squeezed lemon juice
7 walnuts, roasted and finely chopped
Salt and freshly ground black pepper
⅔ cup (160 ml) extra-virgin olive oil

Salad
1 pound (450 grams) carrots, peeled and sliced into matchsticks
1 pound (450 grams) kohlrabi, peeled and sliced into matchsticks
1 pound (450 grams) celery root, peeled and sliced into matchsticks
½ pound (225 grams) beets, peeled and sliced into matchsticks
2 medium tart apples, such as Granny Smith, cored and sliced into matchsticks
½ cup (50 grams) walnuts, roasted and coarsely chopped
2 orange, peeled, pith removed, and thinly sliced
2 to 3 stalks of parsley, chopped

Prepare dressing: In a small pot over medium heat, bring orange juice to a boil. Reduce heat and simmer until orange juice reduces by half. Set aside to cool.
Transfer cooled juice to a blender, and add honey, lemon juice, walnuts, salt, and pepper. Blend until smooth. Pour in oil and mix until a velvety vinaigrette forms.

Prepare salad: In a medium bowl, combine carrots, kohlrabi, celery root, beets, and apples. Pour in dressing and toss gently to coat. Transfer to a serving dish, top with walnuts, orange slices, and parsley, and serve.

Quinoa and Dried Fruit Salad
Yair Feinberg, Fein Cuisine

Nutritious, refreshing, and full of flavor, this salad is distinct and colorful.
Serves 10

Salad
2 cups (340 grams) quinoa
2 cups (480 ml) water
Salt and freshly ground black pepper
1 cup (100 grams) dried cranberries or currants
1 bunch chives, chopped
Handful fresh mint leaves, chopped
⅓ cup (40 grams) roasted slivered almonds

Dressing
¼ cup (60 ml) raspberry or red wine vinegar
2 tablespoons honey
2 tablespoons natural pomegranate or blueberry concentrate
⅔ cup (160 ml) extra-virgin olive oil

Prepare salad: Rinse quinoa in cold water until water runs clean. Transfer to a large pot, add water, salt, and pepper, and bring to a boil over high heat. Reduce heat to low, cover, and cook until quinoa softens, about 1 hour. Add more water if necessary. Transfer quinoa to a large bowl and set aside to cool completely. Mix in dried cranberries, chives, mint, and almonds.

Prepare dressing: In a small bowl, combine vinegar, honey, pomegranate concentrate, and oil. Pour dressing over salad and toss gently to coat. Cover and refrigerate for a few hours before serving, to allow quinoa to absorb flavors.

  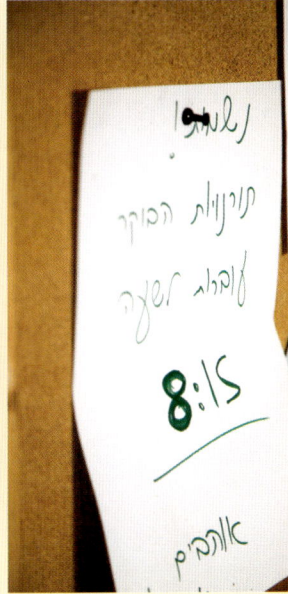

The Wheel Goes Round

In was raining steadily, and he could barely make out the elderly woman standing at the side of the road. Even in the fading light of dusk, however, he realized that she needed help. He stopped his beat-up car in front of her luxury car, got out, and approached her.

In spite of the smile on his face, the woman looked worried. Nobody had stopped for her in the past hour. Would he hurt her? He looked quite poor, not exactly someone you could trust.

He noticed her concern. The way she stood shivering; she might have been trembling from the chilly rain, but she seemed to be shaking a bit from fear, too.

"Can I give you a hand, ma'am," he said. "Looks like you have a flat tire. Why don't you wait in the car while I see what's wrong. By the way, my name is Brian Anderson."

It really was just a flat tire, and Brian crawled under the car, looking for a place to attach the jack. He spent several minutes under the car, but eventually managed to change the wheel. He was quite dirty when he finished, and his hands were sore from working in the cold air.

As he screwed in the nuts on the spare wheel, the woman inside the car opened the window and started talking to him. She told him she was from St. Louis, and just passing through. She thanked him several times for stopping to help, saying it was a real act of kindness.

"How much do you want me to pay?" she asked.

Brian smiled, and said he wouldn't consider taking money. "I didn't stop to make money," he said, "I just saw you were in trouble, and wanted to help."

The woman insisted on paying him something, and Brian said that if she really wanted to, she could simply help out the next person she met who seemed to be in need. Then he stood on the side of the road, brushed off his pants, and waved good-bye as she drove off. It was a cold and dismal day, but Brian had a good feeling in his heart, as he got back in his car and headed home.

Several miles down the road, the woman stopped at a roadside café to have something to eat before she continued on her journey. The café was dingy and dirty, with two old fuel pumps located in front of it. A waitress approached the elderly woman, bringing a clean towel with her so the woman could dry off her wet hair. The woman noticed that the waitress was pregnant. She also noticed that the waitress's shoes were quite worn, and didn't look very comfortable. If the woman was suffering from a sore back or tired feet, it certainly didn't show in her manner. 'How a person with so little could give so much to another human being,' the woman marveled to herself as she ordered a bowl of hot soup. Then she remembered Brian Anderson.

The woman ate her soup, asked for the bill, then paid with a $100 dollar bill. When the waitress returned with the woman's change, she found the woman had left already, leaving a note on the napkin. The note said: "You don't owe me anything. I was in the same situation as you, and someone helped me as I am helping you. If you really want to pay me back, just continue the chain of love and caring." Under the napkin were four more $100 bills.

When the waitress was home that night and in bed, she thought of the money and the woman's note. How could that woman have known how much she and her husband needed the money? Her husband, who was now sleeping beside her, had been so worried. Now he could relax a bit. She kissed her husband softly as he slept, and whispered in his ear, "Everything will be alright. I love you Brian Anderson."

Salads

Appetizers for the Shabbat Table
Aviv Moshe, Messa

Four of the recipes below can be prepared in advance; the fifth is best seasoned just before serving. Together, these salads add a blush of bright color to the traditional white Shabbat tablecloth.

Cooked Olive Salad
Serves 10

2 tablespoons extra-virgin olive
8 cloves garlic, peeled and sliced
2 pounds (900 grams) green olives, pitted, and well rinsed
1 carrot, peeled and cubed
3 stalks celery, chopped
¼ teaspoon red chili powder
1 teaspoon ground cumin
½ cup freshly squeezed lemon juice
3½ ounces (100 g) tomato paste
1 tablespoon sweet paprika, in oil
4 cups water

In a medium frying pan, heat oil over medium-high heat. Add garlic and olives and cook for about 3 minutes. Add carrot, celery, chili powder, and cumin, and sauté for 5 minutes.
Add lemon juice, tomato paste, and paprika. Pour in water, and bring to a boil, then reduce heat to low and simmer for about 20 minutes. Serve warm or at room temperature.

Greek Eggplant Salad
Serves 10

3 medium eggplants, peeled and cut into ¼-inch rounds
Salt
Olive oil, for frying and drizzling
2 Bermuda onions, peeled, halved lengthwise, and thinly sliced
3 red bell peppers, roasted, peeled, seeded, and cut into strips
5 pickles, cut into thin strips
½ cup fresh parsley, chopped
Lemon juice

Sprinkle eggplant slices with salt, place in a colander, and let sit for 3 hours, to draw out liquid. Shake gently to remove salt.
In a large frying pan over medium-high heat, heat a generous amount of oil. Add eggplant and sauté until golden. Transfer to a plate lined with paper towels to absorb excess oil.
In a mixing bowl, combine onions, peppers, pickles, and parsley. Season with lemon juice, oil, and salt. Arrange eggplant pieces on a large serving dish, top with onion mixture, and serve.

Roasted Vegetable Salad
Serves 10

3 Bermuda onions, peeled and coarsely chopped
1 pound (450 g) cherry tomatoes
1 small hot green chili pepper, sliced into thick strips
3 red bell peppers, seeded and coarsely chopped
3 green bell peppers, seeded and coarsely chopped
Olive oil, to coat
2 tablespoons chopped fresh parsley
2 tablespoons chopped fresh celery leaves
Salt
Freshly squeezed lemon juice

In a medium bowl, combine onions, cherry tomatoes, chili peppers, and peppers. Add olive oil and toss to coat.
Heat a barbecue grill to medium-high, or set oven to broil. Transfer vegetables to barbecue grill, or arrange in a single layer on a large baking sheet. Grill until lightly scorched.
Transfer vegetables to a mixing bowl, and add parsley, celery leaves, salt, and lemon juice. Toss gently to coat.

לך לך

Roasted Hot Pepper Salad
Serves 10

10 red bell peppers, roasted, peeled, seeded, and cut into strips
5 hot green chili peppers, roasted, peeled, seeded, and cut into strips
3 cloves garlic, chopped
Salt
Freshly squeezed lemon juice
Extra-virgin olive oil
½ teaspoon ground cumin

In a large serving bowl, combine roasted peppers, garlic, salt, lemon juice, oil, and cumin. Mix and serve.

Cherry Tomato Salad with Scallions
Serves 10

2 pounds (900 grams) cherry tomatoes, quartered
2 cups scallions, chopped into rings
1 hot green pepper, seeded and chopped
2 tablespoons pomegranate concentrate
Extra-virgin olive oil
Salt
Freshly squeezed lemon juice

In a large mixing bowl, combine cherry tomatoes, scallions, hot pepper, and pomegranate concentrate. Add oil, salt, and lemon juice to taste. Serve immediately.

Mend the World

One day, while a scientist sat working, his seven-year-old son came up to him and asked if he could help him. The scientist was angry at being disturbed, and tried to get the boy interested in something else. When he saw that his efforts were failing, he looked for something to occupy the child.
The scientist tore a page out of a magazine with a map of the world on it, and cut it into pieces. He gave the pieces to his son, along with a roll of tape.
"You enjoy doing puzzles," said the scientist. "Take this torn image of the world, and see if you can fix it."
The scientist thought it would take the boy ages to assemble the puzzle, but after just a few hours, his son called him.
"Dad!" said the boy, "I finished the puzzle!"
The scientist was amazed. He couldn't believe that a seven-year-old child could assemble a puzzle of a map that he had never seen before. He got up from his work, and went to see what the child had done.
"How did you do it?" he asked. "You didn't know what the world looked like."
"You're right," the child said, "I didn't know what the world looked like. But when you tore the page out of the magazine, I noticed a picture of a human being on the other side of the page. When you told me to mend the world, I tried but couldn't. So I turned over all the pieces of paper and mended the human being instead. When I succeeded in mending the human, I saw that I had succeeded in mending the world."

Salads

Roasted Eggplant and Pepper Salad, with Tahini
Daniel Zach, Carmella Bistro

The ingredients in this salad are laid side-by-side on the serving dish. To serve it properly, draw the serving spoon through each element on the plate.
Serves 10

3 medium eggplants, roasted over an open flame
¼ cup (60 ml) extra-virgin olive oil
3 cloves garlic, crushed
5 red bell peppers, roasted, peeled, seeded, and cut into thick strips
3 hot green peppers (optional)
6 tablespoons (90 ml) prepared tahini
Salt and freshly ground black pepper
½ cup fresh parsley, chopped

Carefully scoop out eggplant flesh, and chop with a knife.
In a small bowl, combine garlic and oil.
To serve, arrange peppers and eggplant on a serving dish. Pour oil mixture and tahini all around. Season with salt and pepper, and sprinkle parsley on top.

Fresh Herb, Cashew, and Lemon Salad
Daniel Zach, Carmella Bistro

Be sure to use fresh herbs to make this salad. You can soak, wash, and dry the herbs a few hours in advance, then refrigerate until you are ready to serve. Add seasoning just before serving.
Serves 10

3 cups fresh parsley leaves
3 cups fresh coriander leaves
½ cup fresh mint leaves
5 cups arugula
⅓ cup (80 ml) extra-virgin olive oil
Juice and grated rind from 3 lemons
Fine sea salt
3½ ounces (100 grams) cashews, roasted and coarsely chopped

Partially fill a large bowl with very cold water and immerse parsley, coriander, and mint leaves. Let herbs soak, then rinse well to remove grains of sand or dirt.
Drain leaves and dry in a lettuce dryer, or between two pieces of paper towel. Chill until ready to serve.
To serve, transfer leaves to a serving dish. Pour in lemon juice and oil, and season with salt. Sprinkle lemon rind and cashews on top, toss gently to coat, and serve immediately.

Listen to a Whisper or Wait for a Rude Awakening

A young, successful company manager was driving around his neighborhood in his new sports car. As he was going quite fast, he kept looking around to make sure that no children jumped out from between the parked cars.

All of a sudden, a flying brick hit the back door of his car. The man slammed on the brakes, and drove in reverse. He jumped out of the car, and caught hold of a child standing by the side of the road. The child looked frightened, and had tears running down his face.

"Who are you?" shouted the driver. "What do you think you're doing?"

The driver grew angrier as he shouted.

"This is a new car! The damage caused by that brick is going to cost me a lot of money! Why did you do it?"

"Please forgive me sir," begged the child. "I am really sorry. I didn't know what else to do. I threw the brick because it was the only way I could get someone to stop."

Tears rolled down the child's cheeks. "It's my brother," the boy sobbed. "He fell out of his wheelchair, and I can't pick him up. Could you please help me put him back into his wheelchair?"

The driver was speechless. He saw the boy's brother lying on the road, picked him up, and put him back in his wheelchair. Then he took out a handkerchief and wiped the boy's wounds.

"Thank you and may G-d bless you," said the child gratefully. The man watched the boy push his brother in the wheelchair back to their house, and walked back very slowly to his car, deep in thought.

The company manager never repaired his car door. He left it dented, as a reminder to himself not to go through life in such a hurry that someone would have to throw a brick at him to get his attention. G-d often whispers to tell us things. When we have no time to listen, He throws a brick at us to get our attention. It is up to us to choose whether we listen to the whisper, or wait for the brick.

Salads

Beet Tahini with Chickpea and Black Lentil Salad
Ayelet Or, OM

Adding beets to tahini enrich its appearance and nutritional value. As for the chickpea and lentil salad, its crispy texture is a wonderful compliment to the smoothness of the tahini.
Serves 10

Tahini
2 medium beets, cooked, peeled, and cut into chunks
1 cup (250 ml) tahini paste
2 cloves garlic, whole
1 teaspoon ground cumin
¼ to ½ cup (60 to 120 ml) water
Salt

Salad
1 cup (200 grams) black lentils, rinsed
1 cup (150 grams) cooked chickpeas, canned or frozen and thawed
3 tablespoons chopped fresh parsley
½ hot red pepper, seeded and chopped
2 tablespoons chopped fresh mint
1 small white onion, chopped
1 teaspoon coriander seeds, roasted and ground
1 teaspoon garam masala
6 tablespoons (90 ml) extra-virgin olive oil
¼ cup (60 ml) freshly squeezed lemon juice
Salt

Prepare tahini: In a food processor, process beets until smooth. Add tahini paste, garlic, cumin, and ¼ cup (60 ml) water, and process. Add more water gradually until texture is thick and creamy. Season with salt.
Prepare salad: Fill a large pot with water and bring to a boil. Add lentils and cook for about 8 minutes, until slightly soft. Drain and set aside to cool.
Transfer lentils to a large bowl, and mix in chickpeas, parsley, red pepper, mint, onion, coriander, garam masala, oil, lemon juice, and salt to taste. Mix gently, to coat.
To serve, spread tahini in a ring on a small serving dish, and top with chickpea salad.

Raw Beet Salad
Shaoul Ben Aderet, Kimmel

Though the beets in this salad pose a danger to the traditional white Shabbat tablecloth, the delicious flavor completely justifies the risk.
Serves 10

10 medium raw beets, finely diced
3½ ounces (100 grams) roasted pine nuts
½ cup chopped fresh coriander
10 prunes, pitted and finely chopped
¼ cup (60 ml) date honey
¼ cup (60 ml) balsamic vinegar
¼ cup (60 ml) pomegranate concentrate
¼ cup (60 ml) extra-virgin olive oil
Salt and freshly ground black pepper

In a medium bowl, combine beets, pine nuts, coriander, prunes, honey, vinegar, pomegranate concentrate, and oil. Season with salt and pepper. Set aside until ready to serve.

חיי שרה

Apio: Root Vegetable Dish
Kochava Manor

This distinct sweet and sour vegetable dish hales from the Jewish Turkish kitchen–Apio is Spanish for celery.
Serves 10

¼ cup (60 ml) canola oil
3 cups (720 ml) boiling water
¼ cup (60 ml) freshly squeezed lemon juice
2 tablespoons sugar
1 teaspoon salt
6 carrots, peeled and sliced on a diagonal into ¼-inch rings
4 celery roots, peeled and sliced into ¼-inch slices

In a flat, wide pot, heat a bit of oil over medium heat. Mix in water lemon, juice, sugar, and salt, then add carrots and celery root. Add more water to cover vegetables, if necessary, and bring to a boil. Reduce heat to medium and cook for about 1 hour, until vegetables soften and there is just a bit of liquid left. Adjust seasoning until flavor is equally sweet and sour. Serve chilled or at room temperature.

Remembering the Good; Forgetting the Bad

Two friends wandering in the desert started to argue. One friend slapped the other's face, and the one who was slapped was very offended. Without saying a word, he wrote in the sand: "My best friend slapped my face today."
They proceeded on their journey in the desert until they reached an oasis. They entered the oasis pool to bathe, and the friend who had been slapped started to sink. His friend quickly rescued him, saving his life. When the man recovered, he carved in a stone: "My best friend saved my life today."
The friend said to him, "When I slapped your face, you wrote it in the sand. Now you wrote what I did in stone. Why?"
To which his friend replied, "When someone hurts us, we should write it in the sand, so that the wind, in its forgiveness, blows it away. When someone does something good to us, we should engrave it in stone, so that no wind can erase it."

Salads

Chickpea Casserole with Ginger, Tomato, and Date Honey
Einav Berman, Assif

This dish combines spicy, sweet, and hot flavors, and provides a non-dairy, vegetarian dish for the Shabbat table. It can be prepared in advance and heated just before serving. Excellent alongside steamed cauliflower casserole (see next recipe) and basmati rice.

Serves 10

1⅓ pounds (600 grams) dry chickpeas, soaked overnight in water
¾ cup (180 ml) olive oil, for frying
5 Bermuda onions, thinly sliced
12 cloves garlic, peeled and sliced
One 8-inch (20 cm) piece ginger root, peeled and chopped
2 small hot red chili peppers, seeded and thinly sliced
10 carrots, peeled and sliced into ½-inch rounds
1 28-ounce (800 grams) can stewed whole tomatoes
5 cinnamon sticks
2 tablespoons coriander seeds
2 tablespoons dill seeds
1 teaspoon cumin seeds
1 teaspoon chili powder
4 cups (960 ml) soup stock or water
Salt and freshly ground black pepper
1 cup (240 ml) freshly squeezed lemon juice
1 cup (240 ml) date honey
2 bunches fresh coriander, chopped

In a medium pot, cover chickpeas with water, and bring to a boil. Reduce heat and simmer for about 45 minutes, until soft. Drain. In a wide frying pan, heat oil over medium-high heat. Add onion and sauté until transparent. Add garlic, ginger, and chili peppers, and sauté gently without browning for about 5 minutes. Add carrots and stewed tomatoes, and cook for 10 minutes.
Add cinnamon sticks, coriander, dill, cumin, chili powder, and cooked chickpeas. Add soup stock, salt, and pepper. Bring to a boil, then reduce heat to medium, and cook for 30 minutes.
Add lemon juice and date honey, and cook for 1 hour. Just before serving, sprinkle coriander on top. Serve warm.

Cauliflower, Pepper, and Citrus Casserole
Einav Berman, Assif

This India-inspired vegetarian dish should be served alongside steamed basmati rice. When served as a dairy meal, it is lovely when accompanied by a dip made from yogurt, scallions, coriander and lemon.

Serves 10

1 cup (240 ml) canola oil
2 heads cauliflower, broken into medium sized florets
2 Bermuda onions, cut into eights
5 red bell peppers, cut into 1-inch squares
12 cloves garlic, peeled and sliced
1 small red chili pepper, seeded and sliced
15 scallions, cut into 2-inch strips
One 6-inch piece of ginger, peeled and chopped
Pinch of grated nutmeg
2 tablespoons coriander seeds
2 tablespoons dill seeds
1 tablespoon turmeric
1 teaspoon cumin seeds
5 tomatoes, peeled and chopped (1 14-ounce (400 grams) can is fine, too)
1 cup (240 ml) orange juice
Juice and rind from 2 lemons
1 cup (240 ml) vegetable broth or water
½ cup (120 ml) date honey
Salt and freshly ground black pepper
1 bunch fresh coriander, chopped
1 bunch fresh parsley, chopped

תולדות

Preheat oven to 350°F (180°C). Pour oil into an oven-safe pot and heat over medium-high heat. Add cauliflower and sauté until slightly golden. Add onions and peppers, and sauté gently without browning, until soft.
Add garlic, chili pepper, scallions, and ginger, and cook for 1 minute. Add nutmeg, coriander, dill, turmeric, cumin, and tomatoes, and cook for 5 minutes. Add orange juice, lemon juice, lemon rind, vegetable broth, and date honey, season with salt and pepper, and bring to a boil.
Transfer pot to oven, and roast uncovered for 25 minutes, until vegetables are roasted.
Sprinkle with coriander and parsley before serving.

Steamed Basmati Rice

This fragrant dish is a perfect platform for serving the cauliflower or chickpea dishes on the previous page.
Serves 10

½ cup (120 ml) olive oil, for frying
4 cups (less than 1 kg) basmati rice
1 tablespoon salt
6 cups (1.5 l) water

In a medium pot, heat oil over medium-high heat. Mix in rice and salt, then add water, and bring to a boil.
Cover pot securely by placing a strip of aluminum foil around the edge, then put lid on top. Reduce heat to low, and cook for 14 minutes. Remove rice from heat and let sit, covered, for 30 minutes.

Criticism and Dirty Laundry

A newlywed couple moved to a quiet neighborhood. The morning after they moved in, the first thing the wife saw was a neighbor hanging her laundry.
"Look at the dirty laundry the neighbor is hanging on her line," she said to her husband. "Maybe she should use different soap. Maybe I can help her by teaching her a thing or two about laundry."
The husband pretended not to hear, and didn't say a word.
The wife repeated her criticism every time the neighbor hung out her laundry. After about a month, the wife was amazed to see the neighbor hang out clean laundry. She said to her husband, "Just look at that! She must have learnt how to do the laundry. Maybe another neighbor taught her."
"No," replied the husband. "I got up early this morning and cleaned our windows."

Fish

Fish

Asian Chreime on a Bed of Couscous
Eyal Lavi, Rokach 73

The addition of coconut cream, ginger, and a special blend of spices, imbues this traditional fish dish with an Asian touch.
Serves 10

Bulgur couscous
3 cups (750 grams) thin bulgur wheat
¼ cup (60 ml) corn or canola oil
¼ cup (120 ml) extra-virgin olive oil
2 leeks, thinly sliced
3 carrots, peeled and chopped into small cubes
6 celery stalks, chopped into small cubes
7 ounces (200 grams) white button mushrooms, chopped
Salt
White pepper
About 6 cups (1.5 l) vegetable soup stock or soup

Fish
3 pounds (1.4 kg) Nile perch filet
¼ cup (60 ml) extra-virgin olive oil
2 onions, halved lengthwise and sliced
4 cloves garlic, crushed
2 red bell peppers, seeded and sliced into strips
2 yellow bell peppers, seeded and sliced into strips
2 green bell peppers, seeded and sliced into strips
1 tablespoon sweet paprika
1 teaspoon hot paprika
8 ripe tomatoes, cut into cubes
Salt and freshly ground black pepper
1 cup (250 ml) coconut cream
Handful fresh coriander leaves, chopped
Handful fresh basil leaves, chopped

Prepare couscous: In a medium bowl, mix bulgur with canola oil, and let sit for 5 minutes. In a medium pot, heat olive oil over medium-high heat. Add leeks, carrots, celery, and mushrooms, and sauté until lightly brown. Reduce heat to low, mix in bulgur, and add 2 cups vegetable broth, salt, and white pepper.
Continue stirring and cooking over low heat until broth is completely absorbed. Add another 2 cups of broth, stir, and continue to cook until broth is absorbed. Add more broth, if necessary, and continue to cook gently until bulgur is al dente. Cover to keep warm, and set aside.
Prepare fish: Rinse fish with cold running water, then dry and cut into 1-inch slices. Set aside.
In a wide pan, heat oil over medium-high heat. Add onions and garlic and sauté until onions are transparent. Add peppers and sauté for another 10 minutes.
Add paprikas and sauté for a few seconds over high heat. Add tomatoes, salt, and pepper, and bring to a boil. Reduce heat and cook at a gentle boil for 10 minutes. Add coconut cream, coriander, and basil and cook over medium heat for 10 to 15 minutes, until sauce is thick.
About 7-8 minutes before serving, place fish pieces in hot sauce, and cook over medium heat until fish is thoroughly cooked. Serve on a bed of couscous.

A Tale of Two Brothers

Once upon a time, two brothers lived next door to each other in two farmhouses, in a village full of lakes and rivers. For forty years, they lived in harmony, sharing their equipment and helping one another whenever they could.

One day, out of the blue, a loud argument broke out between the two brothers. In just a few minutes, the argument escalated, and for the first time ever, the brothers stopped talking to each other. Their cooperation ended. A small misunderstanding had turned into giant argument, and this led to harsh words and silence.

One morning, the older brother heard a knock on his door. When he opened the door, he saw a man standing there with a carpenter's tool-box in his hand.

"I am looking for a few days of work," said the carpenter.

"Good," said the brother, "I happen to have some work for you. Look across the river, at the end of the farm, and you will see the farm that belongs to my younger brother. Until a week ago, the only thing dividing our farms was a field, but my brother took a bulldozer and made a river between our farms. He probably did it to annoy me, but I want to show him that I'm the boss. I want you to build a 10-foot wooden fence so that I can't see him and his farm anymore."

"I think I understand," replied the carpenter. "Just show me where the wood is, and I'll get started."

The older brother showed the carpenter the wood, handed him a tin of nails, and set off to do some errands. In the meantime, the carpenter started working. He took measurements, began sawing, and soon started hammering.

At dusk that day, just as the carpenter was finishing his work, the older brother returned home. He stared at the carpenter's work, unable to utter a word.

There was no fence in sight. Instead he saw a bridge that stretched from one side of the river to the other, from his field to his younger brother's field. There were great handrails on both sides of the bridge.

The older brother was still staring when he caught sight of his younger brother, holding out his hands to him at the far end of the bridge.

"You really are a wonderful person," said the younger brother, "to have built this bridge after all the nasty things I said to you."

Both brothers stood still for a moment, at opposite ends of the bridge. Then they walked towards each other until they met in the middle. First they clutched each other's hands, then they embraced. The older brother turned, and saw the carpenter preparing to leave.

"Hey," he shouted. "Stop! Stay for a few more days. I have more work for you!"

"I'd be happy to stay," replied the carpenter with a smile, "but I can't. I have many more bridges to build."

The next time you get into an argument with someone, look for a way to build a bridge, rather than put up a wall or fence.

Fish

Noodles and Frika with Slices of Fish, Chimichurri, Tomatoes and Pickled Lemons
Golan Gorfinkel, Dallal

Frika, also known as farik or fareek, is a form of green wheat that has a smoky flavor. In this recipe, it is combined with thin noodles, and served with fresh fish.

Serves 10

Fish
3 pounds (1.4 kg) fresh Nile perch filets, cut into 1-inch pieces
1 cup flour
Salt and freshly ground black pepper
Soya oil, for deep frying
½ cup (120 ml) extra-virgin olive oil
7 cloves garlic, peeled and cut lengthwise
4 medium onions, chopped
10½ ounces (300 grams) thin egg noodles
1 pound (450 grams) frika (smoked wheat) rinsed and dried
1 tablespoon crushed coriander seeds
4 cups (1 liter) basic fish broth (see facing column)
¼ cup (60 ml) freshly squeezed lemon juice
2 tablespoons chopped fresh mint leaves
16 fresh sage leaves

Chimichurri
5 medium tomatoes, peeled, and cut into small cubes
2 tablespoons chopped pickled lemon
3 tablespoons chopped parsley
5 tablespoons extra-virgin olive oil
½ teaspoon salt

Prepare fish: Mix together flour, salt, and pepper in a large plate. Roll cubes of fish in mixture to coat.
In a large frying pan, heat soya oil over medium-high heat. Working in batches, fry fish until lightly golden. Set aside fish, and discard oil.
Pour olive oil into frying pan, and heat over medium-high heat. Add garlic and onions and sauté for a few minutes, until transparent. Add noodles and sauté until onions and noodles are golden.
Add frika and continue to sauté for about 2 to 3 minutes, mixing occasionally. Season with salt and pepper, and add half the coriander.
Mix in fish, then pour in enough fish broth to cover.
Bring to a boil, then mix in sage, mint, and lemon juice. Cover, reduce heat to low, and simmer for 10 minutes. Remove from heat and let mixture sit, covered, for another 10 minutes.
Prepare chimichurri: In a large bowl, mix together tomatoes, pickled lemon, parsley, oil, and salt.
To serve, transfer fish to a serving dish, distribute chimichurri on top, and sprinkle with remaining coriander.

Basic Fish Broth
Select a saltwater fish if possible, and place fish head, skeleton, and skin in a pot. Pour in enough water to cover, then bring to a boil over medium high heat. Reduce heat to medium and cook at a soft boil for 20 minutes. Strain using a fine mesh strainer.

The Butterfly (attributed to Henry Miller)

A little boy went to visit a clever elderly man, who was his guru. When the boy arrived, the man was holding something in his hand and looking at it very closely. The boy approached the man to see what he was looking at.

"What do you have in your hand?" asked the child.

"It's a butterfly cocoon," replied the man. "Very soon the cocoon will open and the butterfly will come out."

The child was impressed, and asked if he could take the cocoon home.

"I'll let you take it home on one condition," replied the man. "You must promise me that when the cocoon starts cracking and the butterfly beats its wings, you won't touch the cocoon. You must let the butterfly get out by itself."

The child agreed and took the cocoon home. He put it on his windowsill, and sat watching. Nothing happened for a while, and then the cocoon started to move. The boy watched the cocoon vibrate, and then split in half. In front of his eyes, he saw a delicate and beautiful butterfly frantically beating its wings against the cocoon's shell in order to get out. The butterfly seemed too weak, and the boy felt it must be suffering. The boy desperately wanted to help.

The butterfly fought on, and the child couldn't take it any longer. Breaking his promise to the elderly man, the boy gently broke the shell meaning to help the butterfly emerge.

Indeed, the butterfly was now able to leave the cocoon, but although it flapped its wings, it was unable to fly. After a few moments of futile flapping, the butterfly fell to the ground, motionless.

The child gently picked up the butterfly, and saw it was dead. He ran back to the elderly man, tears flowing down his cheeks, and showed him the dead butterfly.

"I understand that you didn't keep your promise," said the man. "Did you let the butterfly emerge from the cocoon by itself, or did you hurry to break the shell?"

"I broke the shell," replied the child. "I couldn't help myself."

"Well, you couldn't possibly have realized the damage you were doing," said the elderly man. "When the butterfly starts beating its wings against the shell, the wings are weak. The only way it can strengthen its muscles is by beating its wings against the cocoon. With every knock of its wings against the shell, the wings get stronger. When you tried to help the butterfly by doing its work for it, you prevented the butterfly from developing the muscles of its wings. That is why the butterfly died."

Fish

Seared Nile Perch in Garlic and Lemon, with Moroccan Salsa
Ayelet Or, OM

Roasted peppers, Kalamata olives, raisins and fresh herbs wrap the Nile perch in delicacies worthy of a queen, and just right for Shabbat, also regarded as a queen.

Serves 10

Salsa
¼ cup (60 ml) extra-virgin olive oil
1 teaspoon ground cumin
½ teaspoon ground cinnamon
½ teaspoon red chili powder or Sudanese pepper
3 red bell peppers, roasted, peeled, seeded, and cut into ½-inch cubes
½ cup Kalamata olives, pitted and chopped
1 Bermuda onion, chopped
5 tablespoons chopped fresh coriander
2 tablespoons chopped fresh mint
¼ cup light raisins
Grated rind from 1 large orange
¼ cup (60 ml) freshly squeezed lemon juice

Fish
2 pounds (900 grams) Nile perch filet, cut into 1-inch cubes
5 cloves garlic, crushed
½ cup (120 ml) extra-virgin olive oil
¼ cup (60 ml) freshly squeezed lemon juice
Salt and freshly ground black pepper

Prepare salsa: In a large frying pan, heat oil over medium heat. Add cumin, cinnamon, hot pepper, and cook until spices 'open', and their flavors are released, and combined.

Place roasted peppers in a medium bowl. Mix in olives, onion, coriander, mint, raisins, orange rind, and lemon juice. Let sit for at least 30 minutes, for flavors to blend.

Prepare fish: Place fish in a non-reactive dish. Combine oil and garlic, pour over fish, and let sit for about 20 minutes.

Drain oil from fish into a large frying pan, and heat over medium-high heat. Add fish cubes, season with salt and pepper, and sauté for about 2 minutes on each side, until fish is thoroughly cooked. Transfer to a serving dish and drizzle lemon juice on top.

To serve, arrange the salsa on top of the warm fish cubes, and serve.

וישב

The Mountain

A father and his son were hiking in the mountains, when suddenly, the son fell and cried out, "Ahhhhhhhhhhhhhhhhh!"
The young man was astonished to hear someone answer him from somewhere on the mountain, "Ahhhhhhhhhhhhhhhh!"
Curious, the son shouted, "Who's there?"
He heard the answer, "Who's there?"
A bit angry at the reply, the son shouted, "Coward!"
In response, he heard, "Coward!"
The son turned to his father and asked him, "What's going on?"
The father smiled and said, "Son, listen to this."
The man shouted into the mountain, "I admire you!"
And the voice answered, "I admire you!"
The man shouted, "You're a champion!"
The voice answered, "You're a champion!"
The man shouted, "You're a success!"
The voice answered, "You're a success!"
The son didn't understand what was going on, so his father explained. "People call this a mountain, but it is actually Life. Life gives you back what you say and do. Life is a reflection of your words and deeds. If you want more love in the world, spread more love around you. If you want happiness, make the people around you happy. If you want a smile, give a smile. This attitude touches every aspect of life. Life will give you back what you give it. Your life is a reflection of yourself. If you don't like what you're getting, look at what you are giving."

Fish

Nile Perch with Lemon and Fresh Herbs
Shaoul Ben Aderet, Kimmel

Make sure you serve this dish with plenty of fresh Challah, so guests can make the most of every drop of sauce.
Serves 10

Fish
2½ pounds (1.2 kg) Nile perch filet, cut into 1½-inch cubes
Juice from 3 lemons
Salt and freshly ground black pepper
Water
4 eggs, beaten
1 cup (100 grams) breadcrumbs
Vegetable or canola oil, for frying

Sauce
1¾ sticks (200 grams) margarine
2 tablespoons chicken soup powder
8 cloves garlic, crushed
1 cup dry white wine
Juice from 3 lemons
Salt and freshly ground black pepper
4 branches fresh rosemary, leaves only, for garnish
10 branches fresh thyme, leaves only, for garnish
1 cup chopped fresh parsley, for garnish

Prepare fish: In a medium bowl, place fish cubes, lemon juice, salt, pepper, and garlic, and enough cold water to cover. Let sit for 20 minutes.
In a small bowl, place eggs. In a separate bowl, place breadcrumbs. Remove fish from marinade, drain, and pat dry with paper towels. Dip fish pieces into beaten egg, then dredge in breadcrumbs.
In a large frying pan, heat a small amount of oil over medium-high heat. Fry fish pieces on each side until golden.
Prepare sauce: In a large frying pan, melt margarine over medium heat. Add soup powder, garlic, wine, lemon juice, salt, and pepper. Bring to a boil, then continue cooking until mixture reduces by half, and a thick sauce forms.
To serve, place fish cubes on a serving plate, and pour sauce over top. Sprinkle rosemary, thyme, and parsley on top, and serve.

Coping with Problems

The daughter of a cook complained to her father about the difficulties of coping with life. Her father took her into the kitchen, and showed her three saucepans full of boiling water. He put a carrot in the first pan, an egg in the second, and grains of coffee in the third.

After a while, he took the carrot out of the pan, and put it on a plate. Then he fished the egg out of the water, and put it in a bowl. Lastly, he strained the coffee beans, and poured coffee into a cup. "What do you see?" asked the father.

The daughter looked on the table and saw the following: the carrot was soft and tender. When she removed the shell from the egg, it was hard-boiled. The coffee had a wonderful aroma and tasted good.

The father said, "This is how different people cope with the same problem. The boiling water is a given for each of the three items. The carrot was hard when it reached the water, but emerged soft enough to mash. The egg started off delicate, but became hard all over. The coffee beans produced a wonderful aromatic brew.

"Which product are you like the most, my daughter? When problems arise, how do you cope with them? Are you like the carrot, which looks tough but loses its strength when times are hard? Are you like the egg, with its delicate nature that hardens when confronted? Or are you like a coffee bean, that makes the most out of a stressful situation?"

Coffee beans are best when immersed in boiling water. In order to become a coffee bean, remember that there is a reason for everything that happens in life. What remains for us is to discover the reason, and learn from it. There is no fault that cannot be turned into an advantage.

Fish

Tuscany Baked Fish
Avi Bitton, Adora

This satisfying dish features the classic Italian combination of fish, tomatoes, olives, and basil.
Serves 10

Juice from 2½ lemons
8 cups (2 liters) water
5 pounds (2.25 kilograms) frozen Nile perch filet (4 pounds (1.8 kg) thawed), cut into 2-inch pieces
2 cups (280 grams) flour
2 teaspoons salt
About ¾ cup olive oil, for frying
5 medium onions, chopped
1 head garlic, cloves separated, peeled, and crushed
2 heaping tablespoons sweet paprika
3½ ounces (100 grams) tomato paste
20 medium tomatoes, cut into ¼-inch cubes
Dried oregano
Salt and freshly ground black pepper
One 28-ounce (750 ml) bottle dry white wine
3 cups (720 ml) water
½ pound (225 grams) pitted black olives (such as Thasos olives)
2 bunches fresh basil, leaves only

Combine lemon juice and water in a large bowl. Submerge frozen fish in mixture, and set aside to thaw. Once fish thaws, drain and pat dry with paper towels.
Combine flour and salt in a medium bowl. Dredge fish in mixture to coat evenly on all sides.
In a large frying pan, heat oil over medium-high heat. Add fish and fry until lightly golden. Remove from pan and set aside.
In a wide-based pan, sauté onions and garlic until golden. Add paprika, tomato paste, tomatoes, oregano, salt, and pepper, and cook for 5 minutes.
Add wine and cook for about 5 minutes, until alcohol evaporates. Add fish, then pour in water until fish is three-quarters covered in water. Cook for about 15 minutes, until fish is cooked through, and sauce thickens a bit.
Just before serving, mix in olives and basil.

ויגש

On the Side: White Beans with Fresh Herbs

This dish is excellent alongside any white fish dish. Try it beside the Tuscany Baked Fish (facing page).
Serves 10

1 pound (450 grams) dry white beans, sorted and soaked overnight in cold water
Water
2 stems fresh thyme, leaves only
1 stem fresh parsley, leaves only
1 stem fresh oregano, leaves only
1 clove garlic, crushed
About ¾ cup olive oil
Salt and freshly ground black pepper

Drain beans, and transfer to a cooking pot. Add enough fresh water to cover, then bring to a boil over high heat. Reduce heat to medium, and cook for about 75 minutes, until beans are soft. Drain and transfer to a serving bowl.
In the meantime, process thyme, parsley, oregano, garlic, and olive oil in a food processor, or chop with a sharp knife, until coarsely chopped.
Mix herb mixture into beans, and season with salt and pepper.

A Pair of Socks (A True Story)

One of the Reichmann brothers passed away, leaving behind a billion-dollar estate. He also left behind two wills, one of which was to be opened immediately after his death, and the other one which was to be opened thirty days later.
One of the requests in the first will was that he be buried wearing a particular pair of socks. The man's children brought the socks to the Hevra Kadisha (Jewish burial society) and asked for their father to be buried in them. The Hevra Kadisha refused their request, explaining that this was against Jewish law. The family said their father had been an observant Jew and a learned man, and must have had an excellent reason for his request. The Hevra Kadisha were unmoved, and adamant in their refusal.
The angry family turned to the rabbinical court, but the rabbi there also refused their request. "Although your father made his request while he was alive," the rabbi explained gently, "he is now in the next world, and will surely understand that it is better to be buried in the dust, without socks."
So, the very wealthy man was buried without socks.
When the thirty-day period had passed, the second will was opened. It said something like this: "My dearest children, without a doubt you have buried me without my socks. I hope you now fully understand that even if someone has millions of dollars in his life, he cannot take anything with him when he dies, not even a pair of socks."

Fish

Nile Perch in Tomato, Pepper, Eggplant and Chickpea Sauce
Meir Adoni, Catit

You can prepare the sauce for this dish on Friday morning. In the late afternoon, heat it until it bubbles, then add the fish and cook for about 3 minutes. Cover the pot, turn off the heat, and let the flavors blend. By the time everyone is ready for their Sabbath dinner, the dish is ready to serve.
Serves 10

Canola oil, for frying
10 sweet red peppers, whole
3 eggplants
4 cloves garlic, crushed
3 dry hot peppers
15 very ripe tomatoes, cut into quarters
1 pound (450 grams) cooked chickpeas, canned or frozen and thawed
6 dried whole sweet red peppers
½ bunch fresh coriander, on the stalk, coarsely ripped
1 bay leaf
Sugar
Salt and freshly ground black pepper
2 tablespoons chopped pickled lemons, for garnish
1 teaspoon ground cumin, for garnish
10 6-ounce (180 grams) Nile perch filets

Roasted peppers: In a large deep frying pan, heat oil over medium-high heat. Add red peppers and sauté until skins brown. Remove from pan, cool slightly, and peel.
Smoked eggplants: Place eggplants on an open flame and sear until skin blackens. Set aside to cool, then remove scorched peel, and place flesh in a large bowl.
Tomato sauce, first stage: In a wide-based pan, heat a little oil. Add garlic, hot peppers, and tomatoes, and cover. Bring to a boil, then reduce heat to low, and simmer for 15 minutes. Transfer mixture to a strainer and press through, to produce a thick, tomato paste. Set aside vegetables in strainer for using in the Swiss Chard Salad (see next page).
Tomato sauce, second stage: In a separate wide-based pan, combine ¼ cup (60 ml) oil and tomato paste, cooking over medium heat for about 3 minutes. Add roasted sweet red peppers, hot peppers, eggplant flesh, chickpeas, and half the coriander. Mix in bay leaf, sugar, salt, and pepper.
Add fish pieces, cover, and simmer over low heat for about 10 minutes. Turn off heat and let fish sit, covered, for another 10 minutes.
To serve, sprinkle pickled lemons, cumin and remaining coriander on top. Serve with fresh challah and Swiss Chard Salad (see recipe facing page).

ויחי

Swiss Chard Salad (for serving alongside fish)

If you serve this salad with a non-meat meal, serve it with thick sour yogurt on the side!

Serves 10

2 stalks Swiss chard
¼ cup (60 ml) olive oil
3 onions, chopped
2 cloves garlic, chopped
1 small hot dried pepper
1 tablespoon ground cumin
¼ cup (60 ml) freshly squeezed lemon juice
Salt and freshly ground black pepper

Separate white and green parts of chard. Cut white stalks into ½-inch chunks, and coarsely chop the green tops.
In a wide-based pan, heat oil over medium-high heat. Add onion, garlic, and hot pepper, and cook until lightly golden.
Add Swiss chard stalks and cook for 15 minutes over low heat, mixing regularly.
Add Swiss chard greens, and cook for 10 minutes. Mix in cumin, lemon juice, salt, and pepper. Serve warm or at room temperature.

The Fisherman

An old Chinese story tells of a fisherman who went fishing every day, and caught only one fish. He took the fish home, ate it with his wife, then went for a walk with her on the banks of the river. At the end of each day, he went to sleep satisfied and content.
One day, the fisherman met a businessman from the West, and the businessman asked him, "Why do you catch only one fish every day? If you spent more time on the banks of the river, you could catch more fish, keep one for yourself, and sell the rest. That way, you could save money and buy property."
"And then what?" asked the fisherman.
"You could do it for many years, and in the end you would be rich."
"And then what?" asked the fisherman.
"Then you could grow old gracefully, eat fish every day, and walk on the banks of the river."

Fish

Mafrum Fish in Eggplant, Tomato Sauce and Tahini
Chanoch Bar Shalom, Chanoch Bar Shalom Catering

In this beautiful interpretation of mafrum, the fish and sauce are cooked separately, and combined just before serving.
Serves 10

Fish
Vegetable oil, for frying
3 eggplants, cut lengthwise into fourths
1 pound (450 grams) skinless Nile perch filet, coarsely chopped
8 cloves garlic, crushed
8 tablespoons chopped fresh mint
8 tablespoons chopped fresh coriander
Salt and freshly ground black pepper

Sauce
1 28-ounce (800 grams) can whole tomatoes, or 2 pounds (900 grams) plum tomatoes, peeled
¼ cup (60 ml) olive oil, plus more for serving
1 large onion, chopped
8 cloves garlic, crushed
3 red hot peppers, coarsely chopped
1 tablespoon tomato paste
Juice from ½ lemon
1 teaspoon sugar
Salt
White pepper
1½ (360 ml) cups prepared tahini, for serving

Prepare fish: Preheat oven to 375°F (190°C). In a large frying pan, heat ¾-inch oil over medium-high heat. Fry eggplant pieces until lightly golden, then transfer to a plate lined with paper towels, and set aside.
In a medium bowl, combine fish, garlic, mint, coriander, salt, and pepper.
Lay eggplant pieces on a work surface, and place fish mixture along one narrow end. Roll up eggplant all the way to the other end. Transfer to a baking sheet, then bake for 5 minutes.

Prepare sauce: Process tomatoes until smooth. In a medium frying pan, heat oil over medium-high heat. Add onion and sauté for 1 minute. Add garlic and sauté for 1 minute. Add hot peppers, tomato paste, lemon juice, sugar, salt, and pepper, and cook for at least 30 minutes, until sauce thickens.

To serve, pour hot sauce onto a serving plate, and arrange eggplant rolls on top. Pour over tahini, and drizzle a bit of olive oil.

The Story of the Nails in the Fence

Once upon a time, there was a boy with a very bad temper. His father gave him a bag of nails, and told him to hammer one nail into the fence around their yard every time he lost his patience or fought with someone.

The next day, the boy hammered 37 nails into the fence.

Over the next few weeks, the boy learned to control himself, and the number of nails he had to hammer into the fence grew smaller every day. He learned that it was easier for him to control his temper than it was to hammer nails in a fence.

One day, the child didn't have to hammer a single nail into the fence. He went to tell his father, who told him to remove a nail from the fence every time he didn't lose his patience.

Time went by, and eventually the child removed all the nails from the fence. He told his father, who took him to the fence and said, "Son, you have done well. But look at the holes left by the nails in the fence. The fence will never be as it was. When you quarrel with someone and say nasty things, you leave behind a wound inside them. Friends are as precious as jewels. They make us smile and encourage us, they are always prepared to listen to us when we need them. They give us support and open up their hearts to us. Always show your friends how much you love them."

Chicken Livers

Chicken Livers

Liver with Onion Jam
Israel Aharoni

This dish is sweet, sour and rich in iron.
Serves 10

½ to ¾ cup olive oil
1 tablespoon fresh thyme leaves
2 pounds (900 grams) onions, thinly sliced
Salt and freshly ground black pepper
3 tablespoons brown sugar
2 cups (480 ml) water
¼ cup (60 ml) plus 2 tablespoons balsamic vinegar
2 pounds (900 grams) cooked kosher chicken livers
4 scallions, finely chopped

Heat oil and thyme in a large Teflon fry pan over medium-high heat until oil is warm. Add onion and sauté for about 5 minutes, until onion is slightly golden.
Add salt, pepper, and brown sugar, and mix while sautéing for about 3 minutes, until onions turn a nice brown color.
Add water and ¼ cup (60 ml) vinegar, and bring to a boil. Reduce heat to low and simmer for 45 minutes, until onions have a jam-like texture. Remove from pan and set aside.
Heat a bit of oil in same pan over medium-high heat. When oil is hot, add livers and sauté until livers are cooked through.
Add remaining 2 tablespoons vinegar and continue to cook while stirring until livers are nicely glazed.
To serve, pile onions on a serving platter, and place livers on top. Sprinkle with scallions.

Chopped Liver
Livnat Family, Shanti House Volunteer and Donor

Nothing compares to this flavorful spread. Some people prefer the texture when it is chilled before processing. Others prefer to process it while the liver is still warm. Whichever way you serve it, be sure to have fresh challah, tangy mustard, sliced pickles or sautéed onions on the side.
Serves 10

3 pounds (1.4 kg) cooked kosher chicken livers
Goose or canola oil, for frying
4 large onions, chopped into medium slices
1 tablespoon demerara sugar
4 hard-boiled eggs
Salt and freshly ground black pepper

In a medium frying pan, heat oil over medium-high heat. Add onions and fry until lightly brown. Add sugar and cook for a few minutes, until sugar melts and onions are brown.
Remove onions from pan and set aside. Add livers and sauté until cooked.
Transfer onions and liver to a food processor. Add hard-boiled eggs, salt, and pepper, and pulse until desired texture is reached.

וארא

The Story of Love

Once upon a time, somewhere on earth, all human emotions and qualities gathered together. They were a bit bored until Madness spoke up and suggested, "Let's play hide and seek."
Curiosity lifted an eyebrow, and asked, "Hide and seek? How do you play hide and seek?"
Madness explained, "I close my eyes and count to a million. You all go and hide. When I finish counting, I'll come look for you."
Enthusiasm danced with Euphoria, and Happiness was so excited that she managed to persuade Doubt and Indifference to play.
However, not everyone agreed to join in the game. Truth preferred not to hide, because at the end of the day, she is always found, anyway. Pride said it was a stupid game, probably because she hadn't suggested it herself.
Madness started to count, "One, two, three…."
The first one to hide was Laziness who hid under the nearest stone. Jealousy hid in Success's shadow, which, after great efforts, was up the highest tree.
Generosity had trouble finding a place to hide, because she thought that every hiding place would be great for one of her friends. A hole in the tree? Wonderful for Modesty. Under a butterfly's wings? Perfect for Sensuality. And so on and so forth, until she found a hiding place in a little ray of sunshine.
Passion hid in a volcano's crater; Love hid in a bush of roses.
Madness finished counting, called out "A million!" and started looking for everyone. Laziness was the first one to be found…only three steps away. The second to be discovered was Doubt, who was found sitting on the fence because he couldn't decide where to hide.
Next, Passion was heard shaking the volcano. Suddenly Jealousy popped out, and Success was discovered. Only Love could not to be found.
Madness looked everywhere. Under every stone, behind every tree, at the top of every mountain. Just as he was about to give up, he saw a rose bush, and peeked between the branches.
Suddenly, there was a whimper! Love's eyes had been scratched by the prickly branches. Madness was devastated, and didn't know how to make it up to her. He apologized, cried, begged for forgiveness. He even promised to accompany her everywhere.
So from that day onwards, Love is blind, and Madness accompanies her.

Chicken Livers

Chicken Livers in Turmeric
Mariuma

Who says kids don't like liver? They'll love this version! Make sure you set aside about 15 minutes for making this recipe, so that you dedicate all your attention to frying the livers, and make sure the sugar browns nicely and doesn't stick to the bottom of the pot.

Serves 10

Olive oil, for frying
6 onions, thinly sliced
4 pounds (1.8 kg) cooked kosher chicken livers
¼ cup (50 grams) plus ½ teaspoon sugar
1 pound (450 grams) white button mushrooms, halved
1 heaping teaspoon turmeric
1 tablespoon chicken soup powder
Salt and freshly ground black pepper
½ teaspoon ground cumin
½ teaspoon ground coriander seeds

In a medium frying pan, heat oil over medium-high heat. Add onions and ½ teaspoon sugar and fry for about 15 minutes, until onions brown.
Add liver, mushrooms, turmeric, soup powder, salt, pepper, cumin, coriander, and remaining ¼ cup sugar. Sauté for about 15 minutes, stirring regularly, until mixture is nicely browned.

Crispy Chicken Liver Salad with Spinach Leaves and Orange Slices
Ayelet Or, OM

This striking dish is juicy, colorful and brimming with freshness.
Serves 10

Liver
½ cup (55 grams) flour
Salt
2 eggs, beaten
1 tablespoon Dijon-style mustard
1 cup (100 grams) breadcrumbs
2 pounds (900 grams) cooked kosher chicken livers
Vegetable oil, for frying

Salad
6 tablespoons sherry or red wine vinegar
1 pound (450 grams) baby spinach leaves
4 oranges, peeled, divided into slices, and membranes removed
1 small Bermuda onion, sliced into thin rings
¼ cup (25 grams) coarsely chopped walnuts
About ½ cup (125 ml) olive oil
Sea salt
3 to 4 tablespoons date honey

Prepare liver: Mix together flour and a bit of salt in a small bowl. In a separate bowl, combine eggs and mustard. In a third bowl, place breadcrumbs.
Dredge chicken livers in flour, then shake off the excess. Dip coated livers in egg mixture, then breadcrumbs.
In a medium frying pan, heat oil over medium-high heat. Add chicken livers and fry on all sides until golden. Remove from pan and transfer to a large mixing bowl.
Prepare salad: Drizzle a bit of vinegar on warm chicken livers. Add spinach, oranges, onion, and walnuts. Season with oil, remaining vinegar, salt, and date honey, and mix gently.
Transfer to a large dish, drizzle with date honey, and serve.

The Power of Cooperation

There was once a rich man who loved horses. He loved them so much that even if he was in the middle of a complicated business venture, he would drop everything if he heard about a horse with a special pedigree for sale, and go to the ends of the earth to see it. If he heard about a horse of spectacular breeding, or one with a pedigree going back generations, he would save no expense in order to acquire the horse, thereby increasing and upgrading the horses in his stables.

One day, the man heard of a big horse show that was to take place in a town far away. He didn't think twice. He selected two of his finest horses-a black horse from Egypt and a lovely gray one from India-harnessed them, and set off.

It was a long journey, but the man enjoyed the ride. As long as the sun was shining, and a breeze ruffled the horses' manes, all was well. Suddenly, the weather changed. The sun was concealed by clouds, and a strong wind started to blow. Rain began falling, and the road became muddy. The horses started acting wild, each pulling in the opposite direction. Within an hour, the man found himself stuck in a puddle with his two valuable horses. Angrily, he took up his whip and started beating his horses, but they were unable to pull the carriage out of the mud.

The man sat in despair, until he saw an old man in shabby clothing drive by in a pitiful cart made of old planks drawn by two scrawny horses. To his amazement, he saw that the two bedraggled horses were managing much better than his valuable pair had managed.

"Stop," shouted the rich man. The old man stopped his cart and asked what was wrong. The rich man told him what had happened during his journey, about the mud and about his horses refusing to budge. He went on to say that the old man's scrawny horses seemed to be worth much more than his valuable ones.

The old man smiled and asked, "Where is the gray horse from?"
The rich man replied, "From India."
"And where is the black horse from?" asked the old man.
The rich man replied, "I bought him in Egypt."
"Now all is clear to me," said the old man. "Both of your horses are very valuable on their own, but together they cannot even pull an old cart. My horses are siblings. They were raised in the same stable, and ate from the same trough. Every time I whip one of them, the other tries harder, to help the first, so that he won't suffer so much. With their cooperation, they are able to cross any hurdle, however hard it is. Each one musters all of its strength to rescue the other from unnecessary suffering.

Your horses are strangers to each other. They don't feel the other's pain. Each one thinks only of himself, and they will never be able to do things together. Only a true friend with a big heart can feel the pain of the other."

Chicken Livers

Croissants Filled with Chicken Liver
Orly Pely Bronstein, Food Writer and Editor, Al Hashulchan magazine

This festive, easy-to-make appetizer is best served immediately after baking. If you want to prepare it in advance, fill the dough, roll it, and freeze it until you are ready to bake.
Makes 24 croissants

Vegetable oil, for frying
2 onions, chopped
2 to 3 stems thyme
¾ pounds (300 grams) kosher cooked chicken livers
⅓ cup (80 ml) dry red wine
2 tablespoons balsamic vinegar
Salt and freshly ground black pepper
3 sheets puff pastry or melawach (Yemenite pastry)
Flour, for dusting
1 egg, beaten, for brushing
3 tablespoons sesame seeds, for sprinkling

In a medium frying pan, heat oil over medium-high heat. Add onion and sauté over low heat, until soft and golden. Add thyme and fry at medium heat for 1 minute.
Increase heat to medium-high, add chicken livers, and sauté for 2 to 3 minutes. Add wine, vinegar, salt, and pepper. Cook for 2 minutes, then remove from heat. Cool, then coarsely chop.
Preheat oven to 350°F (180°C) and line a baking sheet with parchment paper. On a lightly floured surface, roll out 1 puff pastry sheet until it is ⅛-inch thick. Cut into 8 even triangles, and brush triangles lightly with beaten egg.
Place a heaping teaspoon of filling along the wide end of each triangle, then roll up into a croissant shape. Gently bend ends inwards. Repeat with remaining 2 pastry sheets, to make 24 croissants.
Arrange croissants on prepared baking sheet. Brush tops with beaten egg, sprinkle sesame seeds, and bake for about 20 minutes, until golden. Serve warm.

בשלח

A Tale of Two Monks

Two monks, a Master and his pupil, left their monastery to visit another one. As is the manner of monks, they didn't waste any time as they went, speaking, eating, and sleeping little.

On the third day of their journey, they arrived at the banks of a river that had overflowed, and met a woman dressed in bridal clothes. "I don't want to wet my bridal gown," the woman said to the monks. "Do you think you could carry me over the river?"

The pupil was about to refuse in the name of his Master, but before he could, the Master put the woman on his shoulders, and carried her across the river.

The pupil watched his Master, but as is the manner with monks, remained silent.

Three days later, the monks drew near the monastery and could see it at the top of the mountain. Before starting up the hill, the pupil stopped and turned to his Master.

"I cannot continue," he said, "until I understand something. How could you take that woman on your shoulders?"

The Master smiled and said, "You have a long way to go until you attain wisdom." "What does wisdom have to do with that woman?" asked the pupil.

"Wisdom is what distinguishes me from you," replied the Master. "I lifted the woman onto my shoulders and carried her for three minutes from one side of the river to the other. After putting her down, I forgot all about her. You, on the other hand, have been carrying her with you for the last three days."

Chicken

Chicken

Chicken Quarters Baked in Parchment Paper
Chanoch Bar Shalom, Chanoch Bar Shalom Catering

This dish features a special technique for making chicken that is particularly juicy and brown.
Serves 10

Juice from 4 lemons
2 lemons, thinly sliced
⅔ cup (150 ml) dry white wine
⅔ cup (150 ml) olive oil
12 cloves garlic, crushed
12 fresh rosemary twigs
4 fresh oregano twigs
2 small hot green chili peppers, seeded and sliced into thirds
Salt and freshly ground black pepper
10 chicken quarters, halved
6 preserved grape leaves, halved, no need to rinse

In a medium bowl, combine lemon juice, lemons, wine, oil, garlic, rosemary, oregano, hot peppers, salt, and pepper. Pour over chicken pieces, cover, and marinate in refrigerator for 2 hours.
Preheat oven to 400°F (205°C). Line a large baking sheet with two sheets of parchment paper, so that the papers overlap in the middle, and the edges of the paper hang out over the edge of the pan. Lay the grape leaves on the center of the parchment paper, then lay the chicken pieces on top, skin side upwards. Fold over edges of parchment paper so that they meet in the middle, then fold together along the top. Staple papers together to make a sealed envelope that keeps steam inside. Place another piece of parchment paper on top, then bake for about 1 hour. Remove top parchment paper and roast for another 20 minutes, or until the paper envelope is completely brown.

Thank you

I dreamt I went to heaven, and an angel showed me around. First, he took me into a large room full of angels. He stopped and said, "This is the reception department. All the wishes that people pray to G-d are received here."

I looked around and saw many angels, sorting pages of paper from all over the world with the wishes that people had requested. We left the room and walked along a lengthy corridor to another room.

"Here," the angel explained, "is the packing and dispatching room. In this room, all the blessings from G-d are sorted, packed, and sent to those who asked for them."

Again, I was very impressed with the activity of so many angels, packing such a large amount of requests from all over the world. We continued down the corridor until we reached the door of a very small room. To my surprise, only one angel sat there.

"This is the acknowledgement department," said the angel with embarrassment. "It is quite sad, really," he added. "So many people get answers to their prayers, and don't even bother acknowledging them."

"And how does one acknowledge a wish received from G-d?" I asked.

"Very simply," replied the angel. "You just say, 'Thank you, G-d'."

Chicken

Maschan
Dror Pilz, Food Writer and Expert on Smoking Meat

This dish, generally served when extended family or friends come for a meal, includes Ras El Chanut, a Moroccan spice mixture that contains paprika, turmeric, fennel, coriander seeds, dried rose petals, nutmeg, salt, and white pepper.
Serves 10

2 cups (480 ml) olive oil
16 large onions, halved and cut into half rings
10 chicken thighs
4 tablespoons Ras El Chanut or baharat (Middle East spice mixture)
5 cups long white rice
1 tablespoon salt
4 cups cooked chickpeas
10 cups chicken broth
3 to 4 large pitas

Preheat oven to 350°F (180°C). In a large, wide-based oven-safe pot, heat a generous amount of oil over medium-high heat. Add onion and sauté until golden. Remove onion using a slotted spoon and set aside. Place chicken pieces in same pot, skin side down. Season with 2 tablespoons Ras El Chanut, and sauté until skin browns.

Turn chicken pieces over, season with remaining 2 tablespoons of Ras El Chanut, and sauté for a few minutes.

Return sautéed onion to pot, to cover chicken pieces. Cover pot, transfer to oven, and roast for 45 minutes. Remove chicken and onion using a slotted spoon, and set aside.

Add rice to pot, and sauté over medium-high heat for about 1 minute. Add salt, chickpeas, and chicken broth, and bring to a boil over medium-high heat. Cover, reduce heat to low, and cook until rice is ready.

To serve, arrange pitas on a large serving plate. Distribute onions and rice on top, then arrange chicken legs all around. Place in the center of the table.

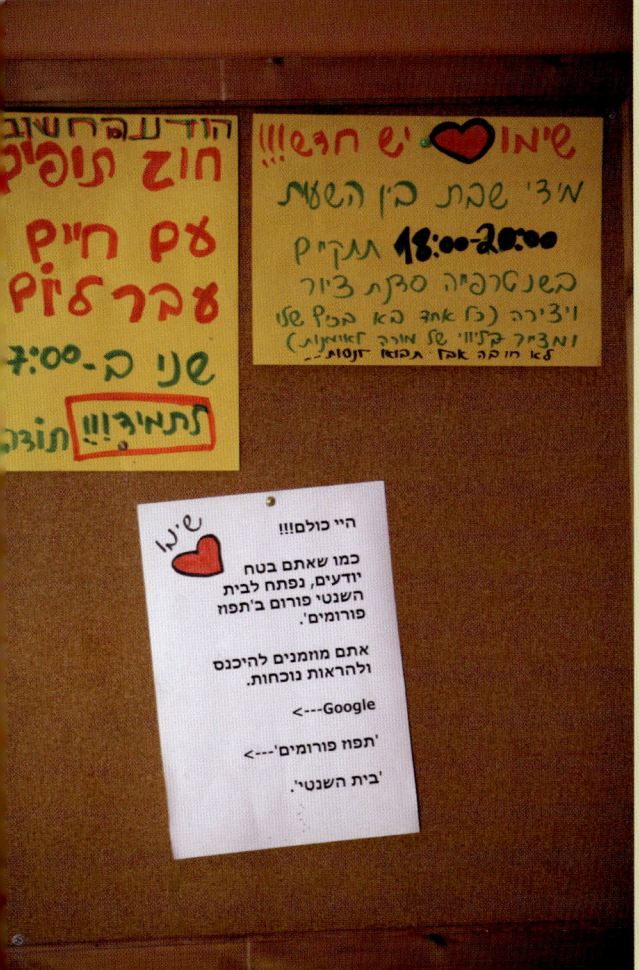

The Painting

There once was a wealthy and distinguished man who happened to have no taste at all. He couldn't even furnish his own home decently, because he couldn't differentiate between Italian and French furniture, and wasn't able to judge if a carpet was cheap or valuable. This shortcoming caused him much unhappiness, and he became a laughingstock amongst his friends.

One day, he saw an announcement in the newspaper advertising the sale of old and rare pictures by famous artists. This gave him an idea. He decided to buy a painting that was so expensive, the art owned by his friends would pale in comparison.

The man hurried to the showroom, but was dismayed when he got there. All the pictures were hanging on the wall, and he couldn't tell the difference between them. He couldn't decide which ones were nice and which ones weren't, and he didn't know what to do. Relying on his own taste was out of the question, and asking experts for advice was beneath his dignity.

He racked his brains trying to find a solution, and finally came up with one. He would simply buy the most expensive painting. He walked around the room until he found the most expensive painting. It looked like a child's scribble, but had a beautiful gold frame. The man purchased the painting immediately. This aroused plenty of attention, and other people in the showroom glanced at the man in admiration. There were even a few journalists who photographed him beside the painting.

That evening, the painting was packed up and sent to his house. Over the next few days, dozens of friends stopped by to admire the treasure. They all praised the painting, and were particularly impressed by the beautiful gold frame. The rich man was delighted. He felt he had finally succeeded.

One day, a prestigious art expert came to the man's house. He went up to the painting, and examined it closely for a long time "It's a very good copy," he said. "Very good indeed."

The rich man was offended. "A copy?" he cried. "How can you say such a thing? I purchased it from a reliable showroom, with notable experts on hand. It cost me a fortune. I don't think they would have cheated me by selling me a copy."

"They didn't cheat you, my friend," replied the expert, "You were not charged for the painting but for its gold frame."

Chicken

Sunday Shnitzel
Razi Livnat, Longtime Shanti House Volunteer

Shnitzel, a traditional favorite among Israeli children, remains popular among Israelis of all ages. At Shanti House, Razi comes every Sunday, preparing about 100 shnitzels every time. Needless to say, there are never any leftovers.

Serves 10

2½ whole chicken breasts (butterflies), pounded and sliced widthwise into 10 thin slices
2 large eggs
2 tablespoons soy sauce
1 tablespoon Dijon mustard
2 cloves garlic, crushed
2½ cups (250 grams) breadcrumbs
¼ cup (25 grams) sesame seeds
1 tablespoon chicken soup powder
1 tablespoon sweet paprika
1 teaspoon salt
1 teaspoon ground black pepper

Canola or soy oil, for frying
1 lemon, cut into wedges, for garnish

In a large, shallow baking dish, beat together eggs, soy sauce, mustard, and garlic. Add chicken breasts, cover with plastic wrap, and marinate in refrigerator for about 1 hour.

In a medium bowl, combine breadcrumbs, sesame seeds, soup powder, paprika, salt, and pepper, then transfer to a shallow dish. Remove chicken pieces from egg mixture and lay them, one at a time, in breadcrumb mixture, so that each side is coated in a thin layer of the mixture. Tap gently to remove excess breadcrumbs, and transfer to another plate.

When all chicken pieces have been coated in breadcrumbs, prepare oil for frying. In a large frying pan, heat ½-inch of oil over medium high heat. Add shnitzels and fry for 2 to 3 minutes on each side, until golden. Transfer to a plate lined with paper towels to absorb excess oil. Serve with lemon wedges on the side.

The Man and the Monkey

One day, a man went for a walk in a forest. He watched the squirrels jump from tree to tree, the birds fly overhead, the animals run around. While he was taking in all the miracles of the forest, a monkey approached him, looking him over from head to toe.

The man politely said, "Hello," and the friendly monkey asked if he would like to accompany him on a trip around the forest.

"I would be delighted," replied the man. "We might even be family. You know, there is a famous human that claims men are descendants of monkeys, so maybe we are cousins."

The monkey showed much interest in his new family member, and with great enthusiasm, he showed the man the most beautiful spots in the forest. As they wandered around, they saw a lion approaching. The man froze on the spot. He looked helplessly at the monkey, who kept his cool, took hold of the man, led him to a nearby tree, and helped him climb up.

The hungry lion waited patiently at the bottom of the tree and said, "I am not budging from here. Decide which of you is coming down, and I promise to let the other one go." The man looked apprehensively at the monkey, but the monkey calmed him by saying "Don't worry. We monkeys do not abandon our friends."

The lion waited patiently, forcing the man and the monkey to sit in the tree for many hours. The man's bones ached, and he was really tired. "We can take turns sleeping," he suggested to the monkey. "One of us will doze for an hour, while the other one stays awake, making sure the one who is asleep doesn't fall off the tree."

The monkey agreed, and the man went to sleep. After an hour, the monkey woke the man up, and fell asleep. While the man was watching the monkey, evil thoughts entered his mind. "If I push the sleeping monkey off the tree," he thought, "the lion will let me go."

The man then pushed the sleeping monkey off the tree, but the monkey immediately woke up, and scrambled up the tree again to the same branch they had been sitting on previously. The monkey didn't utter a word.

Eventually, the lion gave up and went away. The monkey helped the man out of the tree, and showed him how to get out of the forest. Before parting ways, the man thanked the monkey for his help, and asked what he could do in return.

"Don't thank me," replied the monkey, "but I would like you to do me a favor. Please stop telling people that we are related. There is no bigger insult than that in the world."

Chicken

Chicken with Artichokes
Nir Tzuk, Cordeliah

This seasonal dish is a sure sign of spring. It's best prepared a day in advance, since the flavors improve over time.
Serves 10

20 chicken thighs
Salt and freshly ground black pepper
Flour, for coating
Vegetable oil, for frying
4 onions, cut into quarters
One 28-ounce (750 ml) bottle dry white wine
7 artichokes, fresh or frozen, cut into quarters
2 whole lemons, scrubbed, seeded, and coarsely chopped
15 garlic cloves, whole
2 tablespoons turmeric
Water

Season chicken thighs with salt and pepper, then dip in flour. In a Teflon pan, heat a bit of oil over medium-high heat. Add chicken thighs and sauté on each side until golden. Set aside.
In a heavy wide-based pan, heat oil over medium-high heat. Add onions and sauté until golden. Arrange chicken pieces on top, then pour in wine and bring to a boil. Reduce heat to medium, and cook for about 5 minutes, until alcohol evaporates. Add artichoke pieces, lemons, garlic, turmeric, and salt and pepper to taste. Add enough water to cover, bring to a boil, and cover with a tight-fitting lid. Reduce heat and cook at a gentle boil for about 45 minutes, until chicken is soft, and has absorbed the flavors of the lemon and artichokes.

Tabchah Balkra'ah: Chicken in Pumpkin and Potatoes
Zevik Laisten, Head Boys' Instructor, Shanti House

This dish is a pearl from the Tripolitan kitchen. Mash the soft pumpkin in the tomato sauce if you like, then rub it on a thick piece of challah.
Serves 10

Canola oil, for frying
1 onion, chopped
2 tablespoons tomato paste
1 tablespoon sweet paprika
1 teaspoon hot paprika
1 teaspoon coarse salt
Water
5 chicken thighs, divided
1 pound (450 grams) fresh pumpkin, peeled, seeded, and cut into 1¼-inch (3 cm) cubes
5 potatoes, peeled, cut into 1¼-inch (3 cm) cubes

In a medium frying pan, heat oil over medium-high heat. Add onion and sauté until golden. Add tomato paste, paprikas, salt, and ½ cup (120 ml) water. Bring to a boil, then cook over medium heat for 5 to 7 minutes, until tanginess of tomato paste can't be tasted.
Add chicken pieces, pumpkin, and potatoes, and enough water to cover. Bring to a boil then reduce heat to medium and cook for about 40 minutes, until pumpkin breaks apart and dissolves into the sauce. (To help this along, you can mash the pumpkin with a fork.) To make sure chicken and potatoes are covered in sauce during cooking, gently tip pot as it cooks; don't stir with a spoon.

תצווה

Respect

In a country somewhere in the world, there was a king who loved hunting, and prided himself on being an excellent marksman. One day, the king heard rumors about a remarkable marksman whose reputation preceded him.

The king was told that this marksman could shoot a cherry off the top of a cake without touching the whipped cream. It was said that when he went hunting, he always shot the animal between the ears, so that its coat would remain intact. In short, he never missed.

The king decided to challenge the marksman to a shooting match. He sent his envoys out to look for him, and when they found him, he agreed to a contest. After arriving at the palace, the marksman and the king set out for the forest where the king's servants set up the target, so they could start the match.

The king raised his weapon, and with much confidence started shooting into the centre of the target. He was a true expert, and shot three bull's eyes, one after the other. The circle in the centre of the range was only a few centimeters in diameter, and the king perforated it completely.

After the King finished, it was the marksman's turn. He stood in front of the target, raised his rifle, and quickly started to shoot. He shot ten bullets, all of which struck the third circle, just above the bull's eye. Unlike the relatively large hole made by the king's three shots, the marksman's ten shots left just a single tiny hole, the exact diameter of a bullet.

As none of the marksman's bullets had struck the centre of the target, the judges declared the king to be the winner. The king was delighted, shook his rival's hand, and invited him to visit the palace. When they were finally alone together, the marksman turned to the king and said, "I am really pleased that you won. However, I just want you to know that I could have easily beaten you. Out of respect, I deflected my rifle and missed the target on purpose."

Chicken

Paella Chicken
Leon Alcalai, Tony Vespa

There is nothing quite like this festive dish, inspired by Spanish paella. Perfect for anyone who delights in smoky flavors.
Serves 10

10 chicken legs, halved
Olive oil
½ pound (225 grams) smoked goose breast, cut into ¼-inch cubes
3 medium onions, chopped
1 red bell pepper, seeded and sliced lengthwise into thin slices
1 yellow bell pepper, seeded and sliced lengthwise into thin slices
1 green bell pepper, seeded and sliced lengthwise into thin slices
3 cloves garlic, chopped
3 large tomatoes, halved
5 cups (1.05 kg) round white rice
1 gram saffron
About 2 teaspoons salt
8 cups (about 2 l) boiling water
3 lemons, sliced into wedges, for garnish
2 scallions, chopped, for garnish

Preheat oven to 350°F (180°C). Season chicken with pepper. In a large, wide-based pan, heat about 6 tablespoons of oil over medium-high heat. Working in batches, sauté chicken pieces on all sides for about 10 minutes. Set aside.

Add about 2 tablespoons of oil to pan, and heat over medium-high heat. Add smoked goose breast and sauté until fragrant. Mix in onions, peppers, and garlic. Grate tomato flesh into pan; discard skins.

Cook tomato mixture until liquids evaporate. Add rice and mix until completely coated in sauce. Mix in saffron, then boiling water, and salt to taste. Bring to a boil over high heat, then transfer to a baking dish.

Arrange chicken pieces on top, skin side upwards. Bake for about 25 minutes, until liquids evaporate, and rice is sticky, but al dente. Turn off heat, open oven door, and let dish sit for about 5 minutes before serving.

If you'd like to prepare in advance, cover baking dish and place on a hot plate, or cover with aluminum foil, and reheat in an oven. Serve with lemon wedges, and sprinkle scallions on top.

כי תשא

The Scottish Farmer and Penicillin

This story is likely an urban legend, but it's heartwarming nonetheless.

Many years ago, a poor Scottish farmer by the name of Fleming was working in his field. He heard a cry for help from a nearby swamp, dropped all his tools, and ran over to see what was happening.

The farmer found a terrified child in the swamp, stuck up to his thighs in black mud, struggling to get out. The farmer saved the boy from the swamp, dragging him out before he sank further.

The next day, a magnificent carriage stopped by the farmer's humble house. An aristocratic-looking gentleman stepped out of the carriage, and introduced himself as the father of the child the farmer had saved the previous day.

"I want to repay you for saving my son's life," said the man.
"I don't want any reward," replied the farmer.
At that very moment, the farmer's son stepped out of the house.
"Is this your son?" asked the gentleman.

"Yes," replied the farmer.
"I will make a deal with you," said the man. "Allow me to grant the same education to your son as I will to my own. If your son is anything like his father, he will grow up to be someone we will both be proud of."

The farmer agreed, and so it came to be that that Alex, the son of a poor Scottish farmer, came to study at St. Mary's, one of the best schools in London. The young man went to medical school, and eventually become famous as Sir Alexander Fleming, the man who discovered penicillin.

The aristocrat who funded his early education was Sir Randolph Churchill. His son later came down with pneumonia, and it was Sir Alexander Fleming's discovery-penicillin-that saved his life. As for the name of the aristocrat's son; why, he was Sir Winston Churchill.

Chicken

Chicken in Apples, Cinnamon and Caramel Sauce
Segev Moshe, Segev and Segev Express

Imagine the aromas of roasted chicken, apple cider, caramel, and cinnamon, mingling at your Shabbat table. Now stop imagining, and start preparing!
Serves 10

Chicken
10 chicken thighs
10 tablespoons olive oil
Coarse salt and freshly ground black pepper
4 large sweet potatoes, peeled and sliced lengthwise
7 Jerusalem artichokes, peeled
4 potatoes, peeled and sliced lengthwise
10 cloves garlic, peeled and sliced
2 hot green chili peppers
1 cup clear apple juice

Sauce
1 cup (200 grams) sugar
5 cinnamon sticks
8 cups (2 l) clear apple juice
3 tablespoons apple vinegar

Preheat oven 320°F (160°C).
Prepare chicken: In a medium bowl, combine chicken, oil, salt, pepper, sweet potatoes, artichokes, potatoes, garlic, hot peppers, and apple juice.
Transfer to a baking pan, cover with aluminum foil, and bake for about 1½ hours. Remove foil and bake for another 15 minutes, until chicken is a deep gold color.
Prepare sauce: While chicken is baking, combine sugar and cinnamon sticks in a small pot. Cook over low heat until a fragrant caramel forms. Immediately add apple juice and vinegar, and bring to a boil. Continue cooking until liquid is reduced and a thick sauce forms. To serve, pour caramel sauce over warm chicken.

The Island

Once upon a time, many years ago, there was an island inhabited by all the emotions, including Happiness, Sadness, Knowledge, and Love. One day, these emotions were told that the island was about to sink. They began preparing themselves to leave. They packed their belongings, and left one by one...all except Love, who decided to wait until the last moment.

When the island had almost sunk, Love started crying for help. She watched as Happiness set sail in his brightly decorated boat and cried out, "Happiness, can you take me with you?"

"No," replied Happiness. "I can't. My boat is full of gold, silver, and diamonds. There is no room for you."

Love asked Pride, who was sailing near the shore in a magnificent boat, for help. "Please help me," Love begged. "No," replied Pride. "You are all wet, and you'll spoil my boat."

Love saw Sadness nearby, floating on a miserable looking raft. "Sadness!" Love cried out. "Please help me and take me with you."

But Sadness also refused, saying she was too sad, and wanted to be on her own. Then Love asked Cheerful to take her, but Cheerful was so busy singing and laughing that she didn't hear Love's desperate cries.

All of a sudden, an old man Love didn't know came into view, and called out, "Come on board," he shouted. "I'll take you."

So Love boarded his boat, and they sailed away.

When they reached a safe shore, the old man let Love off the boat and went on his way. Love had been so grateful and distracted during the trip that she had forgotten to ask the name of the old man who had saved her.

She found Knowledge, and asked the name of the man who had helped her.

"That was Time." replied Knowledge, knowingly.

"Time?" said Love. "I wonder why Time saved me."

Knowledge smiled and said, "Only Time can appreciate the greatness of Love."

Chicken

Pal'u - Bukharin Rice Dish
Ofira Gordon, Longtime Shanti House Volunteer

This Bukharin dish is festive and satisfying. It can be prepared with or without chicken, and is as appealing to the eyes as it is to the palate.
Serves 10

4 cups (1 kg) round rice, well rinsed
Water
½ cup (120 ml) canola or corn oil
10 chicken pieces (thighs or drumsticks)
4 large onions, peeled, halved lengthwise, and thinly sliced
10 carrots, peeled and cut into matchsticks
2 tablespoons salt
1 tablespoon freshly ground black pepper
2 tablespoons sugar

In a large bowl, place rinsed rice with enough water to cover. Set aside for 30 minutes, to soak.
In the meantime, heat oil in a wide-based pot over medium-high heat. Add chicken, season with salt and pepper, and fry on all sides. Cover and cook over high heat for about 10 minutes. Remove chicken with a slotted spoon, and transfer to a plate. Set aside, covered, to keep warm.
Return pot to heat, and add onion. Sauté over medium heat until transparent. Mix in carrots, salt, pepper, and sugar. Bring to a boil, cover, and cook for 10 minutes.
Arrange chicken pieces in pot in a single layer on top of the vegetables. Drain rice from soaking water and add to pot. Level out rice with the back of a spoon, pour in enough water to cover rice by 1 inch of water. Bring to a boil. Cover pot with a kitchen towel, then place lid on pot, to make it airtight. Reduce heat to low, and cook for 30 minutes.
Remove mixture from heat and let sit for 10 minutes, for rice to finish steaming.
To serve, invert contents of pot onto a serving dish, so that the chicken, onion, and carrots are on top.

פקודי

Bank of Time

Let's do an exercise in reasoning. Your bank announces a campaign that may end at any moment. Every morning they will credit your account with $86,400. You can do whatever you like with the money, but there are a few restrictions:

The money remains in your account for the entire day, but no longer than that.

Whatever you didn't spend during the day will be taken away that night.

You cannot save it, keep it, lend it, or give it away.

You can only use the money for your own needs the same day.

If this really happened, how would you handle it? It is reasonable to assume that you would try to use every single dollar. You wouldn't leave one penny in your account. You might even work out what you would do with it in advance. You would no doubt invest it in the best things possible, not taking any risks, because you wouldn't know when the campaign is due to end.

Is there such a bank in real life? Indeed there is. It is a bank where everyone has an account. However, this bank doesn't give us money, it gives us something far more precious: time!

Every morning, when we open our eyes, we are given 86,400 seconds. This time is given to us to do whatever we like until the end of the day. Whatever time we don't use is wasted. It cannot be saved for another day.

What is the best thing we can do with this time? We can dedicate our time to the most important things. We can arrange our day to make the most of every moment. A second that goes by never returns.

If you want to appreciate the value of a year, ask a student who has been kept behind a grade.

To know the value of a month-ask the mother of a premature baby.

To know the value of a week-ask the editor of a weekly magazine.

To know the value of an hour-ask someone who is waiting to meet their lover.

To know the value of a second-ask the person who was saved from a road accident.

To know the value of a thousandth of a second-ask an athlete who won a gold medal.

Time waits for no one. Yesterday is history, tomorrow is unknown. Today is a gift.

Chicken

Coco: Grandma Ora's Roast Chicken
Ora Ben Yosef, Former Shanti House Housemother

Grandma Ora used to make this dish for the children of Shanti House. In thanks, they gave it its name. Over time, it has become a favorite of the children of children who have stayed at Shanti House.

Serves 10

- 2 whole chickens, quartered
- 1 potato, peeled and cut into 1-inch thick matchsticks
- 2 large onions, cut into ½-inch rings
- 3½ ounce (100 grams) tomato paste
- 2 cups (480 ml) water
- 1 tablespoons chicken soup powder
- 1 tablespoon hawayij (Yemenite soup spice)

Preheat oven to 400°F (205°C). Rinse chicken pieces under running water, then place in a baking pan. Arrange potatoes and onions all around.

In a medium bowl, combine tomato paste, water, soup powder, and hawayij. Pour mixture into pan, cover with aluminum foil, and bake for 2 hours.

The Tools from Hashem (A True Story)

I wanted to make my father happy more than anything in the world! I wanted to bring home a "Very Good" mark from school instead of "Poor" or "Needs Improvement" but I couldn't do it.

One Saturday, when I was in the sixth or seventh grade, my father and I were home alone, and I decided to talk to him about it. I wanted to tell him how sorry I was that I couldn't make him happy by getting good grades like my sister. He listened, looked at me affectionately, and gave the most amazing lecture I have ever heard in my life.

"Fathers don't love their children because they get good marks at school," he began. "Fathers love their children because that's the way it is. You are in my bloodstream. You are in my soul. I love you because you are you.

When G-d created this world, he gave each of us different tools. To one, he gave beauty. To another, he gave dexterity. To another, he gave talent for music or proficiency in math. We have no idea why G-d does what he does. We also cannot blame anybody for the fact that G-d did not give him this or that tool. We can only blame those who do not use the tools that G-d gave them. Don't complain about what G-d didn't give you. Take the time to recognize the tools he did give you. Have patience, and eventually you will see what tools you have."

I loved my father so much that day. This quietly wise man knew all of this long before anybody talked about dyslexia or learning difficulties.

A year or two later, I found the tools G-d had given me. I was sitting in class, and a substitute teacher was teaching. As usual, I was far away. Suddenly, the teacher was standing by my desk.

"What are you doing?" she asked.

"Doodling," I answered.

"And what did you doodle?" she asked

"I drew you, standing by the door," I answered.

The substitute teacher took my drawing and put it in her bag. I later learnt that she had taken the drawing home and shown it to her father, a famous painter.

A few days later, this painter came to our house. He looked at some of my other drawings, and told my parents that they should do everything they could to help me develop my artistic talent.

What can I tell you? From that day on, my father worked day and night to send me to study with the best artists, both in Israel and abroad. Today I am 42 years old, and last month I held my 28th exhibition, this time at the Museum of Modern Art in New York. And what does my father, now a pensioner, have to say about my success? He says "What's all the fuss about? The child found his tools, and is using them."

ויקרא

Chicken

Chicken Stuffed with Ground Meat and Rice
Mariuma

This recipe is easy to prepare, and filled with goodness. To make the most of this dish, add potatoes, zucchini, and carrots to the baking pan.
Serves 10

2 whole chickens
Water
Canola oil, for frying

Glaze
2 tablespoons honey
2 tablespoons sweet paprika
½ cup (120 ml) olive oil
Salt and freshly ground black pepper

Filling
2 cups (400 grams) Persian rice
Water
½ cup (120 ml) olive oil
1 onion, chopped
½ pound (115 grams) ground beef
½ pound (115 grams) ground mutton
½ cup chopped fresh parsley
1 cup (100 grams) pine nuts
2 tomatoes, finely chopped
Baharat (Middle East spice mixture)
Ground cumin
Ground coriander seeds
Salt and freshly ground black pepper
Dry parsley flakes
Sweet paprika
1 tablespoon honey

Place chickens in a pot, with enough water to cover. Bring to a boil over high heat, then boil for 20 minutes. Drain.
In a large pan, heat canola oil over medium-high heat. Add chickens and sauté until brown on all sides. Transfer to a large bowl.
Prepare glaze: In a small bowl, combine honey, paprika, olive oil, salt, and pepper. Rub on chicken to coat thoroughly.
Prepare filling: In a medium pot, combine rice with enough water to cover, and bring to a boil. Cover and cook for about 7 minutes, until parboiled. Drain.
Preheat oven to 320°F (160°C). In a medium frying pan, heat olive oil over medium-high heat. Sauté onion until golden. Add beef and mutton and sauté while mixing until meat changes color. Mix in parsley, pine nuts, tomatoes, baharat, cumin, coriander, salt, pepper, parsley flakes, paprika, and honey. Add parboiled rice, mixing until combined.
Fill chickens with rice mixture and place in a baking pan. Arrange extra filling all around, then cover pan with aluminum foil, and bake for about 1½ hours. Increase temperature to 480°F (250°C), remove aluminum foil, and cook for 30 minutes, until chicken browns.

Life

They were married for many years but were unable to have children. Years passed, but they never gave up hoping that one day they would be able to hold a child of their own in their arms, a child that would compensate for all the years they had waited to hear children's laughter in the house. They were full of hope.

One day, they were rewarded. Their joy knew no bounds! The doctors said that in a few months time, they were going to be parents.

The months that followed were full of joy, expectation, and fear. Finally, and at long last, the husband found himself waiting outside a delivery room. He waited for hours until finally the door of the delivery room opened and a doctor in a white coat, came out.

"I am happy to tell you," said the doctor, "that you have a baby son who weighs 7 pounds 2 ounces. However," the doctor continued, "I am sorry to tell you that your son is suffering from a fatal disease."

"What do we do now? Is there no hope at all?" asked the father in a choked voice. "I regret to have to tell you that whoever suffers from this disease is doomed to die," replied the doctor.

"In the meantime you can take care of him and bring him up to live life the best he can for as long as he has."

The father gulped, then gained the courage to ask, "Maybe you can tell the name of the disease, and I will look for a cure," he said.

"Life!" replied the doctor. "That is the name of the disease, and whoever has it eventually dies from it."

Chicken

Chicken Stuffed with Rice, Mushrooms, and Fresh Herbs
Omer Miller, Dining Hall Restaurant

This classic family recipe is excellent for serving family or guests. If you want to upgrade it, tuck some fresh rosemary, oregano, and thyme branches between the skin and chicken breast.

Serves 10

2 whole chickens

Chicken
4 cups (less than 1 kg) long basmati rice
Olive oil, for frying
4 onions, chopped
2 teaspoons baharat (Middle East spice mixture)
1 teaspoon ground cinnamon
Salt and freshly ground black pepper
6 cups (1.5 l) water
4 cups (about 1 kg) chopped white button mushrooms
1 cup (100 grams) pine nuts, roasted

Marinade
1 cup (240 ml) honey
1 cup (240 ml) orange juice
4 sage leaves, chopped
2 thyme stalks, leaves only
2 oregano stalks, leaves only, chopped
8 cloves garlic, crushed
4 slices lemon
1 hot green chili pepper, seeded and chopped
2 tablespoons sweet paprika

Prepare chicken: Soak rice in a bowl with water for 30 minutes; drain.
In a large, wide-based pan, heat oil over medium-high heat. Add onions and sauté until golden. Add rice, baharat, cinnamon, salt, pepper, and water, and bring to a boil. Cover, reduce heat to low, and cook for 18 minutes.
Preheat oven to 350°F (180°C). In a Teflon pan, heat oil over medium high heat. Add mushrooms, and sauté until golden. Season with salt and pepper, and mix in cooked rice and pine nuts.
Prepare marinade: In a medium bowl, combine honey, orange juice, sage, thyme, oregano, garlic, lemon slices, chili pepper, and paprika. Rub on chickens, inside and out.
Fill chickens with rice mixture, and arrange in a large baking pan. Cover with aluminum foil, and bake for about 1 hour. Remove foil and bake for another 30 minutes, until chickens are brown.

The King Who Had Four Wives

Once upon a time there was a king who had four wives. His fourth wife was his favorite. He spoiled her with beautiful clothes, and always brought her the tastiest foods to eat. Only the best was good enough for her.
The king also loved his third wife very much. He always presented her to the neighboring kingdoms, but in his heart, he was always scared she would leave him for another.
He also loved his second wife very much. He always told her what was worrying him, and asked her advice in solving problems. The king's second wife was kind, thoughtful, and patient. Her advice was wise, and she supported him when times were hard.
The king did not love his first wife, even though she was loyal and worked hard to preserve his kingdom and riches. Indeed, despite the fact that she loved him very much, he hardly paid her any attention.
One day, the king fell ill and knew his time had come. He contemplated his life and wondered, "I have four wives, yet when I die, I will be alone."
So the king said to his fourth wife, "I have loved and spoiled you more than anyone. Now that I am dying, will you accompany me?"
"No way," she replied, and left without another word. Her reply pierced his heart like a knife.
The king asked his third wife, "All my life I have loved you, and have always presented you to everyone. Now that I am dying, will you accompany me?"
"No," she replied. "Life is too good. When you die, I shall remarry."
His heart sank.
The king turned to his second wife. "I have always turned to you for help," he said, "and you were always there for me. When I die, will you accompany me?"
"I'm sorry, but this time I can't help you," she replied. "I can accompany your body to its grave, but I will not be buried with you." Her reply hit him like a bolt of lightening.
Suddenly, he heard a voice. "I'll go with you. I'll follow you anywhere."
The king turned, and saw a skinny woman, the result of years of neglect; his first wife.
"Now, I understand that I should have treated you better when I had the chance," the king said sorrowfully.
We all have 'four wives' in our lives. The fourth is our body. No matter how much time or effort we invest in it, it leaves us when we die. The third is our possessions. Status, money, riches-they all go to others when we die. The second is our family and friends. It doesn't matter how much they were there for us in our lives, they can only accompany us as far as the grave.
The first is our soul-it follows us everywhere, even if we neglect it in our race for money, power, and other pleasures in life.
Strengthen and spoil your soul, because it follows you everywhere.

שמיני

Chicken

Chicken with Potatoes and Red Peppers
Mariuma

This easy-to-make recipe uses staples that are found in most kitchens. Most important of all, it is delicious. If you want to cut down on the amount of fat, skip the initiation frying stage.

Serves 10

¼ cup (60 ml) canola oil
10 chicken legs
8 medium potatoes, peeled and cut lengthwise
3 tablespoons olive oil
3 onions, coarsely chopped
5 heads garlic, divided into cloves
3 red peppers, seeded and cut into large cubes
1 tablespoon turmeric
1 tablespoon chicken soup powder
1 teaspoon ground cumin
1 teaspoon ground coriander seeds
Salt and freshly ground black pepper
4 cups (1 liter) boiling water
1 bunch fresh parsley, chopped for garnish

In a medium pan, heat canola oil over medium-high heat. Add chicken legs, and fry on all sides until golden. Remove chicken legs from pan and set aside. Add potatoes, and fry until golden. (This stage can be skipped if you want to reduce the amount of oil).
In a wide-based oven-safe pot, heat olive oil over medium-hot heat. Add onions, garlic, and peppers, and sauté for 3 to 5 minutes, until golden. Stir in chicken pieces, potatoes, turmeric, soup powder, cumin, coriander seeds, salt, and pepper. Pour in boiling water, and bring to a boil. Cover, reduce heat to low, and cook for about 1 hour.
Preheat oven to 320°F (160°C). Transfer pot to oven, and bake for 30 minutes. Sprinkle with parsley before serving.

Chicken in Coconut Sauce
Mariuma

This dish is a favorite among young guests to our Shabbat table, thanks to its subtle sweetness. If you like, replace the chicken with beef.

Serves 10

6 tablespoons olive oil
6 onions, finely diced
10 cloves garlic, chopped
4 carrots, peeled and chopped into small cubes
8 celery stalks, chopped into small cubes
15 chicken legs, or 3½ pounds (1.6 kg) beef, cut into 2-inch chunks
One 29-ounce (375 ml) can coconut milk
1½ cups (360 ml) water
1 teaspoon soup powder
½ teaspoon ground cumin
1 tablespoon English peppercorns
¼ teaspoon grated nutmeg
2 tablespoons dried basil
Salt and freshly ground black pepper

In a medium pot, heat olive oil over medium-high heat. Add onions and garlic, and sauté over high heat for 3 minutes, until golden. Add carrots and celery, and sauté for a few minutes. Add chicken or beef pieces, and cook for 5 to 6 minutes.
Pour coconut milk and water into pot, and add soup powder, cumin, peppercorns, nutmeg, basil, salt, and pepper. Bring to a boil over high heat, then cover, and reduce heat to low. Cook for about 1 hour, if you are preparing chicken, or 1½ hours if you are preparing beef.

תזריע

No Price for Love

A sign hung in a pet shop: "Puppies for Sale". A little boy came into the shop and asked how much a puppy costs. The seller replied, "Between $30 to $50."
The boy reached into his pocket, took out some coins, and counted out $2.70.
"Can I see the puppies?" asked the boy.
The man smiled and whistled. From the back of the store, a dog and five beautiful puppies ran out. One of the puppies stayed behind.
"Why is that puppy limping?" ask the boy.
The man said that puppy was born with a problem in his leg, and will limp for the rest of his life.
"That's the puppy I want," said the boy said happily.
The store owner was surprised. "If that's the puppy you want," he said, "I'll give it to you as a gift."
The boy was angry, and said, "I don't want you to give me a present. This puppy costs money, like all other puppies. I'll give you what I have now, and every month, I'll give you another 50 cents to finish paying for it."
"Are you sure you want this puppy?" the store owner asked. "It will never be able to play, jump, and run like the other puppies."
The boy bent down, raised his pants leg, and showed the owner a splint that was supporting his own leg. He said to the man. "I can't run either. This puppy needs someone who can understand him.
Tears came to the man eyes, and he said, "I hope and pray that every puppy in my shop finds someone to love it the way you will love this puppy."

Chicken

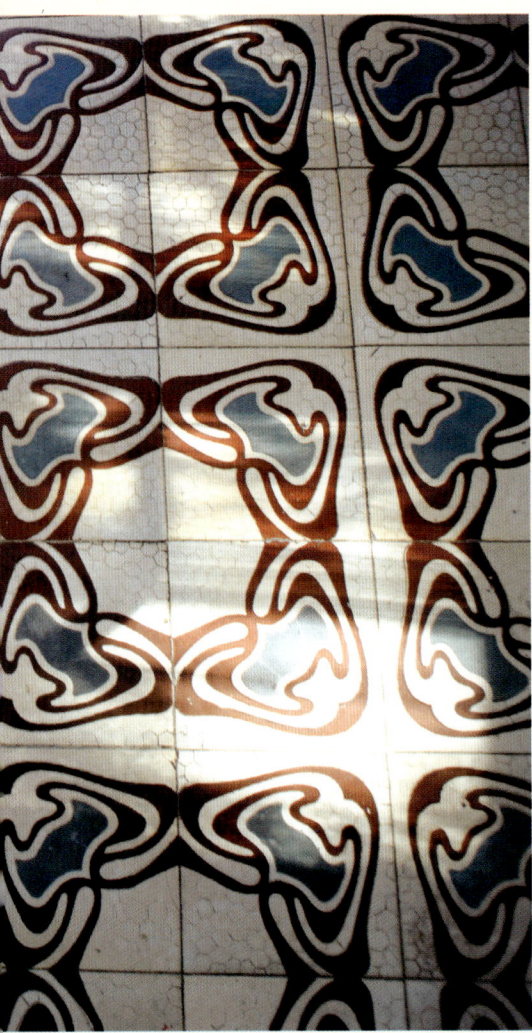

Chicken Stew with Israeli Couscous and Vegetables
Nitzan Raz, Sushi Samba

Israeli couscous is similar to pasta, and has a nutty, toasted flavor. It can be replaced in this recipe with risoni.
Serves 10

1 cup olive oil
4 pounds (1.8 kg) boneless chicken legs or thighs, cut into 1-inch cubes
2 onions, cut into ½-inch cubes
2 leeks, cut into ½-inch cubes
7 potatoes, peeled and cut into ½-inch cubes
2 sweet potatoes, peeled and cut into ½-inch cubes
2 carrots, peeled and cut into ½-inch cubes
1 pound (450 grams) Israeli couscous
Ground cumin
Coarse salt
Freshly ground black pepper
Turmeric
Sweet paprika
Hot paprika
3 cups boiling water

In a large pan or stew pot, heat olive oil over medium-high heat. Add chicken pieces and sauté for about 10 minutes, until golden. Remove chicken from pot, and set aside. Add onions and leeks, and sauté until golden. Add potatoes, sweet potatoes, and carrots, and sauté for 8 minutes.
Mix in Israeli couscous, and sauté for 2 minutes.
Return chicken to pot, add cumin, salt, pepper, turmeric, paprika, and boiling water. Mix well, cover, and cook over low heat for 20 minutes.

The Policy of Monkeys

Start with a cage that contains five monkeys. Using a string, tie a banana to the top of the cage, and put a ladder underneath.

After a while, one of the monkeys will start climbing up towards the banana. The moment he touches the banana, direct a stream of cold water on the rest of the monkeys.

Soon, another monkey will try his luck, with the same results. Every time one monkey reaches for the bananas, the rest receive a cold shower.

Very quickly, the monkeys will learn to stop any monkey that tries to reach the banana.

Now, stop using water. Take one monkey out of the cage and replace him with a new monkey. The new monkey will see the banana and want to climb up the ladder. However, to his surprise and disgust, the other monkeys will attack him when he tries. One or two more attempts will make it very clear to the monkey that if he tries to climb the ladder, he'll be attacked.

Now take another monkey out from the original five and replace him with a new one. This one will also be attacked when he approaches the ladder. Even the previous new monkey will join in the attack.

In the same way, replace the third, fourth, and fifth monkey. Each time the newest monkey tries to reach the banana, he will be attacked. Eventually, and even though all of the monkeys will join in on the attack, none of the monkeys will know why they don't want the new monkey to go up the ladder.

After the original five monkeys have been replaced, there are no longer any monkeys who received the cold jet of water. Still, none of them will allow another monkey to approach the ladder, nor will they approach the banana themselves.

Why not?

Because as far as they are concerned, that's the way things have always been.

This, my friend, is how societies create policy.

Chicken

Citrus Chicken Thighs
Israel Aharoni

Browned slices of chicken, with just the right amount of sweetness. Aromatic and delicious.
Serves 10

10 chicken thighs
6 tablespoons olive oil
½ cup freshly squeezed apple juice
⅓ cup (80 ml) freshly squeezed lemon juice
2 tablespoons freshly grated orange zest
2 tablespoons freshly grated lemon zest
2 tablespoons peeled and grated fresh ginger
2 tablespoons fresh thyme leaves
¼ cup (60 ml) soy sauce
¼ cup brown sugar
Salt and freshly ground black pepper

In a large bowl, combine oil, juices, orange and lemon zests, ginger, thyme, soy sauce, sugar, salt and pepper. Add chicken pieces, skin side down, then cover with plastic wrap and refrigerate for a few hours.
Preheat oven to 400°F (205°C). Transfer chicken pieces to a large baking pan, skin side up. Pour marinade over top, and bake for 40 minutes, basting occasionally.

אחרי מות

The Golden Cage

A king was walking in one of his forests one day, when he heard a wonderful song, a sweet and gentle song that filled his heart. It was the song of the nightingale, which made all the inhabitants of the forest happy.

The king ordered his servants to catch this wonderful singing bird, and bring her to the palace so that she would sing only for him. The servants obliged, and brought the bird to the palace. The king ordered a golden cage be contributed for it, and placed the cage, and the bird, in his garden.

The nightingale was given the very best food, and her cage was placed in an area protected from wind and sun. The nightingale was placed in the cage, and she immediately began singing, from sunrise to sunset. All the people in the palace were happy.

The other palace birds heard about the nightingale's special treatment, and grew jealous.

"Fate has dealt you a good hand," they said to the bird. "You've got a golden cage, the sun and wind don't bother you, and your food is brought to you on a silver platter. Aren't you the lucky one."

"Is that what you think?" asked the bird painfully. "I'm not lucky at all. I'd give up all this in a moment if only I could be free again. I'd trade places with any of you if only I could fly away."

Her words shamed the other birds, who then asked how they could help her. The nightingale told them that she had a sister in a nearby forest that was wiser than all the other birds. "Please find my sister and ask her to advise me what to do."

The birds searched high and low for the sister, and finally found her singing on the branch of a particularly high tree. They told her about her sister, and when they finished, the bird fell from her perch to the ground.

The birds returned to the nightingale in the golden cage, and related what had happened to her sister. The nightingale's face fell, and she stopped singing, eating and drinking.

The people in the palace realized that the nightingale's days were numbered. Indeed, after a few days, they found her lying motionless at the bottom of the cage. The king's servants removed her from the cage and threw her to the ground.

Suddenly, the bird came back to life, singing loudly, and flying gracefully. The bird immediately flew off, found her sister, and thanked her for the good advice.

"Pretend you're dead and then you'll get your freedom back."

Chicken

Chicken with Sweet Potatoes, Soy Sauce, and Honey
Mariuma

The combination of sweet potatoes with soy sauce, and garlic with honey simply can't be beat. Make sure you use real soy sauce for this recipe, and not soy-flavored sauce.

Serves 10

5 tablespoons olive oil
10 onions, chopped
1 teaspoon sugar
12 garlic cloves, whole
10 chicken legs (thighs and drumsticks)
½ cup (120 ml) high quality soy sauce
3 tablespoons honey
1 tablespoon chicken soup powder
1 tablespoon English peppercorns
Salt and freshly ground black pepper
4 large sweet potatoes, with peel, sliced into thick rounds
2 cups (480 ml) boiling water

In a large oven-safe pot, heat oil over medium-high heat. Add onions and sauté until golden. Add sugar and garlic and sauté for 5 minutes, until golden. Add chicken and sauté until golden. Mix in soy sauce, honey, soup powder, peppercorns, salt, and pepper. Arrange sweet potatoes and chicken pieces in alternating layers in the pot. Add boiling water, and bring to a boil. Reduce heat to very low, and cook for 30 minutes.
Preheat oven to 350°F (180°C). Cover pot with aluminum foil, transfer to oven, and bake for 1 hour. Reduce heat to 212°F (100°C), and bake for 1 more hour. Increase heat to 480°F (250°C), remove aluminum foil, and roast until brown.

The Large Stones of Life

A well-known lecturer was asked to give a talk entitled "Planning our Lives Efficiently" to an audience composed of top managers from one of the biggest companies in America. The lecturer stood at the front of the room, looked at his audience, and said, "We are going to perform an experiment."
He took out a large glass container and placed it in front of his audience. Then he took out a dozen large stones, each one about the size of a tennis ball. He place them one by one in the container, and when he couldn't fit another stone, he asked his audience, "Is the container full?"
"Yes," they replied.
The lecturer paused, "Really?"
Then he bent down again and took out a bag of gravel. Carefully, he poured the gravel onto the stones, then shook the container slightly. The gravel sank to the bottom of the container, fitting itself around the stones.
The old man looked up and asked, "Is it full now?"
By now, his audience had begun to understand what was happening, and one of them answered, "It would appear not to be."
"Right," replied the professor. He bent down again, this time bringing out a bag of sand.
He poured the sand into the container, filling the spaces between the gravel and the bigger stones.
Once again, the lecturer asked whether the container was full.
This time, and with no hesitation, all the members of the audience answered, "No!"
"Quite right," replied the lecturer, and he took the jug of water in front of him, and poured it into the container until it reached the brim.
The lecturer raised his eyes to his audience again and asked, "What important truth have we learned here?"
One of the managers said, "We have learned that however full our diaries seem to be, if we really try, we can always fit in another appointment or commitment."
"No", replied his teacher. "The important truth we have learned here is that if we don't fill the container with the big stones first, we'll never be able to fit them in later."
Silence filled the room as each person tried to understand the significance of what he had just heard.
The lecturer looked at his audience and said, "What are the big stones in your lives? Your health? Your family? Your friends? Fulfilling your dreams? Fighting for what you believe in? Taking time for yourselves? Relaxing? Remember to put the big stones in the container first, because if you don't, you're liable to miss out on your lives.
If you place too much importance on the small things in life—the gravel and the sand—you won't have any room for the important things in life. But, if you start with the important things, you can always find room for the gravel and the sand."
Don't forget to ask yourselves, "What are the big stones in my life?" Once you recognize them, put them into your container first.

קדושים

Chicken

Chicken Drumsticks Filled with Pickled Lemons, Lentils, and Rice
Chanoch Bar Shalom, Chanoch Bar Shalom Catering

This aromatic dish is especially impressive. For variety, replace lentils and preserved lemons with 3½ ounces (100 grams) of currants and three large onions, chopped and sautéed until brown.

Serves 10

20 chicken drumsticks, deboned (ask butcher to remove the bone, leaving a small pocket in each drumstick)

Stuffing
1½ cups round rice
3 cups (720 ml) water
1 cup lentils, preferable black
1½ cups chopped fresh herbs (such as parsley, mint, and coriander)
9 ounces (250 grams) preserved lemons, chopped
1 tablespoons grated and peeled fresh ginger
5 cloves garlic, crushed
½ cup (50 grams) roasted slivered almonds
¼ cup (60 ml) olive oil

Marinade
3 tablespoons date honey
3 cloves garlic, crushed
Salt and freshly ground black pepper
⅓ cup (80 ml) olive oil
⅓ cup (80 ml) freshly squeezed lemon juice
⅓ cup (80 ml) dry white wine
3 stalk thyme or rosemary
20 cinnamon sticks

Prepare stuffing: In a medium pot, combine rice with water. Bring to a boil over medium-high heat, then cover, reduce heat, and cook for 20 minutes. Remove from heat and set aside, covered, for about 30 minutes.

In a separate pot, combine lentils with enough water to cover. Bring to a boil over medium heat, and cook for abut 30 minutes, until soft.

Preheat oven to 400°F (205°C). In a medium bowl, combine rice, lentils, fresh herbs, preserved lemons, ginger, garlic, almonds, and olive oil. Stuff mixture into drumsticks, then use a toothpick to seal the hole to prevent filling from spilling out during baking.

Prepare marinade: Rub date honey and garlic on drumsticks, season with salt and pepper, and arrange in a baking dish. Pour oil, lemon juice, and wine all around, then sprinkle with rosemary. Roast for 40 minutes, until brown.

To serve, remove toothpick and insert a cinnamon stick into the opening of each drumstick.

אמור

The Clock

A woman in a small town worked as a telephone operator. She worked all alone in her office, connecting customers to the numbers they requested. She never complained about her work, and took pride in learning to identify her clients by voice.

Some of her customers called regularly in order to ask the time of day. In a corner of her office stood a large clock, and she used it to tell time.

There was one caller she especially liked. He called every day, just before midday, at exactly the same time.

"Hello Madam," he would say politely. "Could you possibly tell me the exact time?"

"The time is five minutes to twelve," she would reply.

"Thank you so much," he would say, and that would be the end of the conversation.

This exchange of pleasantries repeated itself day after day, season after season, year after year. It was a fixture in the life of the operator, as the polite caller never missed a day.

Eventually, it was time for the operator to retire. Her last day at work was very emotional. She answered her calls even more cordially than usual, and said a warm goodbye to her regular clients. She waited in growing anticipation for just before midday, when the polite gentleman always called.

"Hello Madam," he said, as always, "Could you possibly tell me the exact time?"

"The time is five minutes to twelve," she said, and continued. "Forgive me for my curiosity, but today is my last day at work. I'm dying to know who you are, and why you phone me every day, at exactly the same time, to ask me the time."

"You know the clock tower in the town square?" the man asked. "I'm the man who rings the bell every day at midday. That's why I have to know the exact time."

The operator laughed and said, "Let me tell you a secret. All these years, I've been setting the clock in my office to the chimes of your clock tower in town square…."

Chicken

Chicken in Raisins and Olives
Rachel Shtark Biniamin, Shanti House Volunteer

Raisins and olives are an unusual, interesting, and delicious combination.
Serves 10

Canola oil, for frying
2 large onions, chopped
16 chicken pieces (drumsticks or thighs)
3½ ounces (100 grams) tomato paste
6 cloves garlic, crushed
½ cup (50 grams) small raisins
½ cup pitted green olives
½ tablespoons chicken soup powder
½ teaspoon sweet paprika
1 teaspoon ground cumin
Water

In a small pan, heat oil over medium-high heat. Add onion and sauté until brown. Add chicken pieces, tomato paste, garlic, raisins, olives, soup powder, paprika, cumin, and water to cover. Bring to a boil, cover, and cook for 30 minutes.

Chicken with String Beans
Mariuma

When string beans are in season, guests at Shanti House wait for this dish with bated breath.
Serves 10

3 tablespoons olive oil
5 onions, finely chopped
5 garlic cloves, whole
2 carrots, peeled and cut into small cubes
1 teaspoon sugar
14 ounces (400 grams) tomato paste
1 tablespoon sweet paprika
1 heaping tablespoon chicken soup powder
1 teaspoon ground cumin
1 teaspoon ground coriander seeds
1 teaspoon ground black pepper
1 teaspoon crushed black pepper
2 cups (480 ml) boiling water
10 chicken legs (thigh and drumstick)
1¾ pounds (800 grams) frozen string beans

In a medium pot, heat oil over medium-high heat. Add onion, garlic, carrot, and sugar, and sauté until onion browns. Mix in tomato paste, paprika, soup powder, cumin, coriander, and pepper, and cook for about 30 seconds.
Pour in boiling water and cook while stirring for 2 minutes. Add chicken pieces and beans, and bring to a boil. Cover pot, reduce heat to medium, and cook for about 1 hour.

The Tree

A beautiful old tree stood proudly alone at the top of a hill. Its fruits were juicy, sweet, and delicious; its flowers had a fragrance which could be smelled from afar; its fresh green leaves shone in the sun.
Only its rough, old, brown trunk felt ugly and useless, for it had neither taste nor perfume. It loved its fruit, flowers and leaves, but was sad and miserable.
One winter day, a strong wind began blowing on a hill. The wind was so strong that it began blowing off the fruit, tearing off the flowers, and scattering the leaves all around. Only the trunk, solid and strong, was indifferent to the wind's force.
However, when the bark saw what was happening to the flowers, fruit, and branches, it tried to hold onto them and protect them.
When the wind saw the strength of the tree's love, it stopped raging and went to blow on another tree.
Each one of us is a fruit, a flower, a leaf, in a world that belongs to all of us. The love we have is the trunk that connects us to each other. This love makes us solid and strong, so that even the strongest wind cannot overcome us.

Chicken

Chicken Legs Stuffed with Almonds and Pistachios
Chanoch Bar Shalom, Chanoch Bar Shalom Catering

Simple ingredients, precise flavors, impressive serving, and just a bit of help from the butcher. The white fava bean spread is a delicacy from the Tripolitan kitchen that can be served at the beginning of the meal, or alongside the chicken.
Serves 10

Filling
½ cup (50 grams) ground blanched almonds
1 slice white bread, crust removed, soaked in water and squeezed dry
8 cloves garlic, crushed
½ cup fresh herbs (such as rocket, parsley, basil)
Freshly grated zest from 1 lemon
⅓ cup (80 ml) olive oil
Salt and freshly ground black pepper
½ cups (50 grams) whole pistachios, peeled

10 chicken legs (thigh and drumstick), deboned (the drumstick bone can be left exposed)
Salt and freshly ground black pepper

Marinade
3 tablespoons honey
5 cloves garlic, crushed
2 tablespoons rosemary, coarsely chopped
⅓ cup (80 ml) dry white wine
⅓ cup (80 ml) olive oil

Preheat oven to 400°F (205°C).

Prepare filling: In a food processor, combine almonds, bread, garlic, and fresh herbs. Process until smooth. Gradually add lemon zest and olive oil, processing until smooth. Season with salt and pepper, and mix in pistachios.

Season chicken pieces with salt and pepper, and lay skin side down on your work surface. Place a bit of filling in the center of each chicken piece, and fold over chicken to enclose. Use toothpicks or kitchen twine to tie chicken piece together. Turn over chicken pieces, and arrange, skin side up, in a baking dish.

Prepare marinade: In a small bowl, combine honey, garlic and rosemary. Rub mixture on chicken pieces, pour wine and oil into baking dish, and roast for 35 to 40 minutes.

בחקתי

White Fava Bean and Olive Oil Spread

½ pounds (225 grams) split white fava beans, soaked for 1 hour in cold water
6 cups (1.5 L) water
¼ cup (60 ml) olive oil, plus more for garnish
4 cloves garlic, crushed
Juice from ½ lemon
½ teaspoon ground cumin
Salt and freshly ground black pepper
1 tomato, grated, or 1 roasted bell pepper, chopped, for garnish

Drain beans, and transfer to a cooking pot. Add water, and bring to a boil, then reduce heat to medium, and cook for about 40 minutes, until beans are completely soft. Drain, and set aside to cool slightly. Transfer beans to the bowl of a food processor, and add oil, garlic, lemon juice, cumin, salt, and pepper. Process until smooth.
To serve, transfer mixture to a small serving dish, top with grated tomato or chopped pepper, and drizzle with oil.

The Cracked Bucket

A village woman had two buckets which she used every day to transport water from the fountain to her home. One bucket was cracked, and the other was whole. The cracked bucket was always half-empty when the woman reached her home; the whole bucket was always full.
For two years, the woman brought one and a half buckets of water home from the fountain. The whole bucket was proud of itself, but the cracked bucket was ashamed. It felt as if it could only perform half of its job.
One day, as the woman drew water from the fountain, the cracked bucket spoke.
"I'm ashamed," said the bucket. "Because of my cracks, water drips the whole way home."
"Don't be ashamed," said the old woman, with a smile. "Have you ever noticed that on your side of the path, there are flowers, but on the other side there are none? I know about your flaw, and that's why I planted flowers on your side of the path. Every day, while we walk home, you water the flowers along the path. Thanks to you, one side of my path is lined with beauty. If you weren't the way you are, the path wouldn't be as beautiful as it is."
Every one of us has some kind of flaw. It is these flaws that make us special, and add beauty to the world.

Ground Meat

Ground Meat

Stuffed Onions
Erez Komarovsky, Erez's Galilee Cooking School

The stuffing in this recipe is made with mashed potatoes rather than rice, for a soft filling. Use regular rather than lean meat to make this dish juicy and moist.
Makes 10 servings

7 large onions
Water, for cooking
3 medium potatoes
1⅓ pounds (600 grams) ground mutton or veal
2 onions, finely chopped
1 bunch fresh parsley, chopped
½ cup finely chopped dill
¼ cup finely chopped mint
1 flat teaspoon English peppercorns
1 teaspoon black peppercorns
1 teaspoon coriander seeds
2 star anise
2 pieces nutmeg peel
4 to 5 tablespoons olive oil, plus more for greasing
Salt
Fresh grape leaves
4 to 6 cups (1 to 1.5 l) chicken stock

Make a deep lengthwise incision that reaches the center of each onion, then place onions in a large cooking pot. Add water to cover and a pinch of salt, and bring to a boil over medium-high heat. Reduce heat to low, and simmer for about 1 hour, until onions are completely soft.
In the meantime, place potatoes in a separate pot, and add enough water to cover. Bring water to a boil over medium-high heat, then reduce heat and cook until potatoes soften.
Remove potatoes, peel, and mash.
In a medium bowl, combine veal, mashed potatoes, chopped onions, parsley, dill, and mint. Using a mortar and pestle, grind English and black peppercorns, coriander, star anise, and nutmeg until finely ground and uniform. Add to veal mixture, and knead until smooth. Knead in oil and salt until smooth.
Drain onions, and separate into layers. Stuff each layer with veal mixture.
Grease a wide-based pot, and line with grape leaves. Carefully place stuffed onions upside-down on leaves. Pour in chicken stock until onions are half covered. Place pot over medium-high heat, and bring stock to a boil. Cover pot, reduce heat to low, and simmer for 1 hour. Check mixture regularly as it cooks, adding more chicken stock if necessary. Serve hot.

A Stranger Came to Stay

I have no idea how it all started. A few years after I was born, my father met a stranger in the street, someone who was new in our small town. My father was charmed by the newcomer, and invited him to come and live with us. The stranger was easily received, and has been with us ever since.
Throughout my childhood, it never occurred to me to question the stranger's position in our home. He had a special place in my thoughts. My parents were wonderful teachers: my mother taught me to differentiate between right and wrong; my father taught me to be precise. The stranger, however, would tell stories.
He enchanted us for hours with all kinds of stories. Adventures, mysteries, comedies. If I wanted to know about politics, history, or science, he knew the answers. He knew about the past and the present, and even seemed able to predict the future. He made me laugh and cry. He never stopped talking, but Dad didn't seem to mind.
Sometimes, my siblings and I would try to shut each other up so that we could hear what the stranger had to say. At those times, Mom often got up, left the room, and went to the kitchen for a bit of peace and quiet. (I wonder, now, if she didn't pray that the stranger would simply disappear.)
Father set out clear moral rules for our household, but the stranger never felt he had to follow them. For example, swearing was forbidden in our home, not only for us, but for everyone who came to visit. Not so for our longstanding visitor, though. He often spoke rudely, using language that made my father cringe and my mother blush.
My father forbade drinking alcohol, but the stranger encouraged us to try. He also told us that cigarettes were cool, cigars were masculine, and pipes were distinguished. He spoke freely about sex, and was often crude and embarrassing.
I now know that many of the errors of my youth were due to the influence of this stranger. Time after time, he defied the values my parents had instilled, but he was never rebuked or asked to leave. More than fifty years have passed since the stranger came to our house…and he's still there. He isn't nearly as charming as he used to be, either. Still, if you enter my parent's room, you'll find him in a corner, waiting for an audience, so he can show off all he can do and say.
What's his name, you wonder? We call him Television
He has a wife, now, of course. Her name is Computer.

במדבר

Ground Meat

Braided Puff Pastry with Ground Beef, Eggplant, and Olives
Michal Moses, Chef and Food Writer

In honor of Shabbat, even traditional stuffed pastry pockets known as burekas are dressed in elegant attire. This beautiful braided dish is impressive and delicious. Serve with grated tomato and tahini.

Serves 10

1 pound (450 grams) puff pastry, frozen and thawed
Flour, for dusting

Filling
A little oil
1 eggplant, peeled and diced into ½-inch cubes
1 onion, chopped
1 pound (450 grams) ground beef
¼ cup dry white wine
½ cup (50 grams) almond flakes or pine nuts, toasted
15 pitted olives, coarsely chopped
½ bunch parsley, chopped
½ bunch coriander or mint, chopped
Ground cumin
Salt and freshly ground black pepper

1 beaten egg, for brushing
Kosher salt, for sprinkling

Preheat oven to 400°F (205°C), and line a baking sheet with parchment paper.

Prepare filling: In a medium pan, heat oil over medium-high heat. Add eggplant, and sauté until golden. Transfer to a plate lined with paper towels to absorb excess oil.

Add onion to pan, and more oil if necessary, and sauté until golden. Stir in beef and sauté, mixing so that that beef stays crumbly, until beef changes color. Pour in wine and cook until liquids evaporate. Remove mixture from heat, transfer to a mixing bowl, and set aside to cool.

Mix in almonds, olives, parsley, coriander, cumin, salt, and pepper. On a lightly floured surface, roll out puff pastry to form a 20 x 8-inch rectangle. Pressing lightly with a knife, draw three lengthwise lines on rectangle, dividing it into three even sections. Do not cut through pastry with the knife.

Place beef mixture in a mound along middle section. Cut thick diagonal lines on left and right sections of pastry, to make several diagonal strips on both sides.

Bring a pastry strip from the right side over to the left side. Bring a pastry strip from the left side over to the right side. Continue in this manner to make a braid of puff pastry that covers the beef mixture. Carefully transfer braided pastry to baking sheet, and brush with beaten egg. Sprinkle coarse salt evenly on top, and bake for 30 minutes, or until pastry is golden. If pastry darkens too quickly as it bakes, reduce heat to 350°F (180°C). Cool slightly before serving.

Be Yourself

One day, while passing by the village fountain, a lion saw a beautiful maiden. The maiden, a farmer's daughter, was walking home with a jar of water on her shoulder, and the lion followed her until she entered her hut. A moment later, the lion roared loudly, causing the girl's father to come out. The farmer saw the terrifying lion, mustered his courage, and asked him what he wanted.

"Your daughter," said the lion. "I want to marry your daughter."

The shocked farmer replied, "Of course, of course you can marry my daughter. But if she sees you like that, she'll die of fright. At least get rid of that awful mane of yours."

The lion went to the best hairdresser in town and had his mane cropped off. Then he went back to the farmer's hut. "Your daughter," he roared. "Immediately."

"Absolutely," replied the farmer. "But those claws of yours. If my daughter sees them, she'll die of fright. Get them cut, and I'll get my daughter ready."

The lion headed off, to find the best manicurist in town. "And don't forget to get rid of that threatening crown at the end of your tail!" added the farmer.

After a while, the farmer heard a roar outside the hut. He came out and looked at the lion. "Just one more thing," he said, this time with a tinge of scorn in his voice. "Your jaw. Those awful teeth. They're not for my daughter. Get rid of them and I'll give you my daughter."

The lion left, and returned to the hut some time later. He tried to roar, but a ridiculous wail emerged instead. "Who are you?" asked the farmer.

"Who am I? I am the lion who has come to marry your daughter."

"Marry my daughter?" said the farmer. "I'd never give my daughter to a creature like you, one who is lacking in form and character, who is willing to give up all the things that make him special!" And with that, the farmer grabbed a broom and began beating the lion.

And the lion, who wasn't really a lion at all, ran away shamefacedly.

Ground Meat

Meatballs in Lemon Sauce
Razi Livnat, Longtime Shanti House Volunteer

This Turkish recipe first surprised the young people staying at Shanti House. Now, it's a favorite. Serve on a bed of steamed rice, mashed potatoes, or couscous.

Serves 10

Meatballs
2 pounds (900 grams) ground red turkey, or ground chicken and beef
4 eggs
3 tablespoons soy sauce
1 bunch fresh coriander, chopped
1 cup (100 grams) breadcrumbs
Vegetable oil, for frying

Sauce
Olive oil, for frying
3 onions, finely chopped
5 cloves garlic, crushed
1½ cups (360 ml) freshly squeezed lemon juice (about 6 lemons)
2 cups (480 ml) chicken stock
8 Swiss chard leaves, cut widthwise
Salt and ground black pepper

Prepare meatballs: In a large mixing bowl, combine turkey, eggs, soy sauce, coriander and breadcrumbs. Cover and refrigerate for 30 minutes.

Prepare sauce: In a small pot, heat about 2 to 3 tablespoons olive oil over medium-high heat. Add onion and garlic, and sauté for about 7 minutes, until transparent. Add lemon juice and chicken stock, and bring to a boil. Add Swiss Chard, salt, and pepper. Cover, reduce heat to low, and let simmer for 10 minutes.

While sauce simmers, shape and fry meatballs: Wet hands and shape mixture into 1-inch balls. In a medium frying pan, heat about 3 tablespoons of olive oil over medium-high heat. Fry meatballs on all sides, until golden. Transfer to a plate lined with paper towels to absorb excess oil.

Transfer cooked meatballs to simmering sauce, and increase heat to medium-high. Bring sauce to a boil, then cover and reduce heat to low. Cook for about 30 minutes, until sauce thickens and meatballs have absorbed the flavor.

בהעלותך

Put Down the Glass Today

The professor began the class by lifting up a glass with a little water inside. He held it high to ensure everyone could see and then asked the students.

"How much do you think this glass weighs?"

"2 ounces!" shouted one student.

"4 ounces!" shouted another.

"¼ pound!" said a third.

"I don't know, actually," said the professor. "In order to know, I would have to weigh it. And I don't plan on doing that. My question is, what would happen if I held the glass like this for a few minutes?"

"Nothing," replied the students.

"And what would happen if I held it like this for an hour?"

"Your hand would start hurting," said one student.

"That's true," replied the professor. "And what would happen if I held it like this a whole day?"

"Your hand would become numb, your muscles would tense up, you might even become paralyzed, and then you'd have to go to the hospital," joked one student. All the others laughed.

"Right!" said the professor. "But during all that time, does the weight of the glass change?"

"No," said the students.

"So what causes the pain and numbness?" asked the professor.

There was an embarrassed silence.

"Let me rephrase the question. What do I have to do to stop the pain?"

"Put the glass down," replied a student.

"Exactly," smiled the professor. "This glass of water is like our daily problems. If we think about them for a little while, that's fine. If we continue thinking about them, it starts hurting. If we carry our thoughts even longer, the pain becomes paralyzing, and we won't be able to function.

It's important to consider the challenges and problems we face in life, but it's more important to let them go at the end of the day, before we go to sleep. That way, we can wake up strong and refreshed each morning, able to face the new challenges each day brings."

So remember, my friends, put the glass down today!

Ground Meat

Vegetables Stuffed with Meat, Rice, and Lentils
Daniel Zach, Carmella Bistro

When this beautiful dish is served, there's no need to put flowers on the table. If you plan to prepare it for Friday night supper, remember to place the lentils to soak on Thursday night. Serve with fresh challah, for absorbing all the sauce.
Makes 10 servings

Vegetables
6 medium red bell peppers
6 medium turnips, peeled
6 medium beets, peeled
6 large Jerusalem artichokes or zucchinis, peeled

Filling
½ pound (225 grams) black lentils, sorted, rinsed, and soaked overnight in cold water
5 tablespoons olive oil
1 large onion, chopped
3 cloves garlic, crushed
½ teaspoon baharat (Middle East spice mixture)
½ teaspoon sweet paprika
½ teaspoon salt
½ pound (225 grams) ground beef
½ pound (225 grams) Persian rice, rinsed
¾ cup chopped fresh parsley

Sauce
Olive oil, for frying
1 medium onion, sliced
3 cloves garlic, crushed
3 medium tomatoes, grated
2 tablespoons tomato paste
1 tablespoon sugar
2 teaspoons sweet paprika
½ teaspoon hot paprika
½ teaspoon ground cumin
½ teaspoon turmeric
8 cups (2 l) clear chicken broth or water
Salt

Prepare vegetables: Using a sharp knife, cut tops off peppers, and carefully remove seeds and ribs. Reserve tops for covers. Cut tops off turnips and beets, and scoop out insides using a Parisian spoon. Leave about ¼-inch of flesh along sides and bottom, and reserve tops for covers. Cut artichokes in half lengthwise. Scoop out insides, leaving a thick layer of flesh along sides and bottom. Set vegetables aside.

Prepare filling: Drain lentils and set aside. In a medium pan, heat oil over medium-high heat. Add onion, and sauté for about 7 minutes, until transparent. Add garlic, baharat, paprikas, and salt, and cook for about 1 minute. Cool slightly, then transfer to a mixing bowl. Mix in beef, rice, parsley, and drained lentils. Use your hands to combine thoroughly.

Prepare sauce: In a large pot, heat oil over medium-high heat. Add onion and sauté until golden. Add garlic, tomatoes, tomato paste, sugar, paprikas, cumin, turmeric, and chicken broth. Bring to a boil, and cook for 5 minutes. Season with salt, if necessary.

Assemble vegetables: Stuff vegetables with filling, and cover with reserved vegetable tops. Arrange in a deep, wide-based pot so that vegetables are close together. Pour sauce into pot, so that stuffed vegetables are about three-quarters covered. Cover pot, and cook over very low heat for about 1½ hours. Serve stuffed vegetables on a slightly concave dish, to contain the sauce.

שלח לך

Invitation

A woman came out of her house and saw three strangers with long white beards sitting in her yard. She said to them, "I don't know who you are, but you must be hungry. Please come into my house and have something to eat."

"Is your husband at home?" they asked.

"No, he isn't. He's out," she replied.

"In that case, we can't come in."

When her husband returned that evening, she told him about the strangers.

"Tell them I'm at home now, and invite them in," he said. So the woman went outside, and asked the men to come in.

"We can't come in together," they said.

"Why not?" she asked.

"He is Riches," answered one of the men, pointing to his friend. "And he is Success," he said, pointing to the other. "I am Love. Now go and talk to your husband. Decide which of us you would like to invite."

The woman returned and related what had happened to her husband.

"Great!" he replied, "Let's invite Riches, and we'll be rich for ever."

The wife didn't agree. "Why don't we invite Success?" she suggested.

Their daughter-in-law, who had been listening to their conversation, made the following suggestion, "Don't you think it would be better if we invited Love. Then our entire house would be full of Love!"

After a moment's thought, the husband and wife agreed with their daughter-in-law, and the wife went outside to speak with the strangers.

"Which one of you is Love?" she asked. "Please come and be our guest."

Love got up and walked towards the house. The other two got up and followed.

"I only asked Love to come," said the woman, surprised. "Why are you two coming also?"

"If you had invited Riches or Success," replied one of the old men, "the other two would have stayed outside. However, wherever Love is invited, Riches and Success follow."

Ground Meat

Meatballs with Baharat and Hawayij
Shaoul Ben Aderet, Kimmel

These meatballs have a distinct Middle Eastern flavor, thanks to the hawayij and baharat.
Serves 10

Meatballs
2 pounds (900 grams) ground chicken or beef
3 eggs
1 cup (100 grams) breadcrumbs
1½ tablespoons baharat (Middle East spice mixture)
1½ tablespoons hawayij (Yemenite soup spice)
5 medium onions, chopped
5 cloves garlic, crushed
1 cup chopped fresh parsley
Salt and freshly ground black pepper
Olive oil, for frying

Sauce
5 ripe tomatoes, grated
1½ tablespoons baharat (Middle East spice mixture)
1½ tablespoons hawayij (Yemenite soup spice)

Prepare meatballs: In a medium bowl, combine chicken, eggs, breadcrumbs, baharat, hawayij, onions, garlic, parsley, salt, and pepper. Cover and refrigerate for 30 minutes.

Wet hands and shape mixture into 1-inch balls. Heat olive oil in a frying pan over medium-high heat. Add meatballs and fry on all sides, until golden.

Prepare sauce: In a large pan, combine tomatoes, baharat, and hawayij. Bring to a boil over medium heat. Add meatballs, reduce heat, and cook gently for 10 minutes.

Pumpkin in Date Honey and Rosemary
Shaoul Ben Aderet, Kimmel

Serves 10

2 pounds (900 grams) fresh pumpkin, peeled, seeded, and cut into ¾-inch cubes
½ cup (120 ml) extra-virgin olive oil
10 cloves garlic, chopped
3 tablespoons date honey
5 rosemary twigs
Salt and freshly ground black pepper

Preheat oven to 400°F (205°C). In a large baking pan, combine pumpkin, garlic, date honey, rosemary, salt, and pepper. Toss gently to coat, then roast for about 30 minutes, until pumpkin is soft.

קרח

On The Quality of Hearing

A husband was worried that his wife's hearing was not what it once was and that she may need a hearing aid. He wasn't quite sure how to approach the subject with her, so he phoned the family doctor for advice. The doctor asked the man to conduct a simple, informal test to help assess the problem.

"Here's what to do," said the doctor. "Stand about 30 feet away from your wife and say something in a normal tone of voice. If she doesn't respond, move a bit closer to her, and repeat what you said, in the same tone of voice. Continue doing this until she responds."

That evening, while his wife was preparing supper in the kitchen, the husband decided to try the doctor's suggestion. He sat in the living room, about 30 feet from his wife, and said, in a normal voice, "Honey, what's for supper?"

There was no reply.

The husband got up from his chair, and began walking towards the kitchen. After a few steps, he repeated his question.

"Honey, what are we having for supper?"

Again, no reply.

The husband walked a few steps closer, into the kitchen by now, and repeated his question. "Honey, what are we having for supper?"

Again, no reply.

The husband entered the kitchen, stood about 6 feet from his wife, and asked again. No response.

He walked right up to his wife, stood behind her, and asked again. This time he got the following answer:

"Isaac, for the fifth time, we're having roast chicken! Didn't you hear me the first four times?"

If we only look at something from one point of view, we can never get the whole truth. Sometimes, things look (and sound!) completely different from another perspective.

Ground Meat

Meatballs on a Bed of Eggplant and Tomatoes
Malca Eliakim, Longtime Shanti House Volunteer

This delicacy brings a bit of Greek flavor to the Israeli Shabbat table.
Serves 10

Eggplant
2 medium eggplants, peeled and sliced into 1-inch thick rounds
Salt, for sprinkling
Flour, for coating
2 to 3 eggs, beaten
Vegetable oil, for frying

Meatballs
2 pounds (900 grams) ground beef
2 eggs
1 bunch fresh parsley, chopped
6 cloves garlic, crushed
Salt
1 teaspoon chili powder

Sauce
9 ounces (260 grams) tomato paste
3 cups (720 ml) water
½ bunch fresh parsley, chopped
1 teaspoon chili powder

3 tomatoes, sliced into ½-inch rounds

Prepare eggplants: Place flour and eggs in separate shallow bowls. Season eggplant rounds with salt, then dredge in flour, and dip in eggs.
In a large shallow pan, heat oil over medium-high heat. Sauté eggplant on both sides, until golden. Set aside.
Prepare meatballs: In a medium bowl, combine beef, eggs, parsley, garlic, salt, and chili powder. Wet hands and shape mixture to form 1-inch balls. Heat oil in pan (add more oil if necessary) over medium-high heat. Add meatballs, and fry on all sides until golden. Transfer to a plate lined with paper towels to absorb excess oil.
Grease a wide-based pot with oil, and line with a layer of tomato slices. Top with a layer of eggplant slices, then with a layer of meatballs.
Prepare sauce: Combine tomato paste, water, parsley and chili powder. Pour mixture into pot, ensuring that meatballs are covered. Bring to a boil over medium-high heat, then reduce heat to medium and cook for about 1 hour.

More Precious Than Diamonds

There was once a diamond merchant, the son of a wealthy and respected family. He was very successful, and lived with his family in a beautiful house with many servants.

The food at their table was always the finest, and their lives were made comfortable with anything and everything that money could buy. From his youth, he was simply used to the very best.

One day, he heard of a diamond fair in a far away city. The merchant decided to attend, even though the journey took several weeks. He hired a driver with a fine carriage and fast horses, filled his purse with money, and stayed at the finest inns along the way, in the most comfortable rooms, just as he was accustomed.

Finally, the merchant arrived at the fair and purchased the diamonds he wanted. The money he had left was just enough for the return journey. He bid farewell to his new business acquaintances, and turned to leave the town. This took him through a market, and he saw, to his astonishment, an old book for sale at one of the stalls.

The book was beautifully illustrated, and although the drawings had grown faint over time, the man remembered it as a book from his childhood, a book from which his mother had read to him often.

The man's heart was filled with longing when he imagined the happiness on his wife's face, and the radiance on his son's face, when he brought home such a book. He would read to them both, and show them the magnificent illustrations.

"How much is the book?" he asked the vendor.

The vendor, who immediately understood the man's excitement, named a price that was probably a hundred times its worth. The merchant, however, quite unlike himself, didn't argue. He put away some money for his return journey and offered the man the rest.

The vendor took the money happily and wrapped the book in a tattered piece of cloth. With the book in hand, the merchant headed home.

When nighttime fell, the merchant looked for lodgings he could afford. He found a cheap hostel, with a miserable straw mattress, and stayed there, after eating a meager meal of dry bread and black coffee. His bones hurt and his body ached, but one look at the book in his bag was enough to give him sweet dreams.

The return journey seemed much longer and more arduous. Every inn was worse than the previous inn, and his money disappeared as his body grew sore.

However, every night, before falling asleep, he would take out the book, undo its wrappings, read a little, and imagine the pleasure it would bring his family. At that moment, his discomfort would vanish with the thought of the value of the compensation to come.

Ground Meat

Meatlovers Meat Sauce
Raphi Aharonovich, Meister Butcher, Yeda Habsarim

Richer than a standard bolognaise sauce, this dish can be served on top of a wide range of dishes. Try it with baked potatoes, mashed potatoes, couscous, or steamed rice.
Serves 10

½ cup (120 ml) olive or canola oil
6 large onions, diced
2 Bermuda onions, diced
8 cloves garlic, crushed
8 carrots, peeled and diced into very small cubes
5 celery stalks, chopped
Salt and freshly ground black pepper
4 pounds (1.8 kg) coarsely ground beef or red turkey
7 ounces (200 grams) smoked goose breast, or 11 ounces (300 grams) smoked turkey pastrami, cut into small cubes
½ pound (225 grams) cooked kosher chicken liver, cut into large cubes
¼ cup (60 ml) tomato paste
½ cup (120 ml) sweet Asian chili sauce
1 tablespoon soy sauce
1 teaspoon sugar
Salt and freshly ground black pepper
½ teaspoon ground cumin
1 teaspoon sweet paprika
½ cup (120 ml) chicken or beef stock
5 scallions, sliced into rings, for garnish
1 bunch fresh parsley, chopped, for garnish

In a large flat-bottom pot, heat oil over medium-high heat. Add onions and sauté gently until slightly golden. Add garlic, carrots, celery, salt, and pepper. Reduce heat to medium, and cook while stirring for about 10 minutes. Transfer vegetables to a heatproof bowl and cover.

Add more oil to pot if necessary, and heat over medium-high heat. Add ground beef, and cook over high heat, stirring constantly, for about 5 minutes, until beef changes color. Add smoked goose breast and liver, and sauté for 5 minutes, until brown.

Return vegetables to pot, and add tomato paste, chili sauce, soy sauce, sugar, cumin, and paprika. Cook over high heat, stirring regularly, for about 5 minutes. Add chicken stock and bring to a boil, then reduce heat to low, cover, and cook for 25 to 30 minutes. Check sauce after 20 minutes. If too much liquid remains, remove cover and cook uncovered for last 10 minutes. Taste and adjust seasoning.

Serve on a bed of rice, couscous, or mashed potatoes. Garnish with chives and parsley.

Path of Life

A child was sitting in a hammock in the garden, staring at the sky. His father approached him and said, "What are you thinking about?"
"I'm wondering what I'll be when I grow up," the child answered very seriously. "What kind of man will I be? What kind of life will I have?"
"Come inside with me," said the father, and they went into a room where there was a play mat with several roads printed on it. The father took a toy car and placed it on one of the roads.
"This is you," said the father, "and this is your life."
"I want to drive," exclaimed the child.
"Good. First rule: The steering wheel is always in your hands, nobody else's. Unfortunately, not even mine."
The child, feeling very important, started driving the car.
"When you're young, you start driving in a straight line."
The child reached a junction and looked at his father, questioningly.
"You'll meet many such junctions in your life. It means you're beginning to grow up. It means it's time to choose. Second rule: You choose where to turn. I can advise you, but I can't choose for you."
"OK," said the child. "I'm going to go straight. But one minute, I don't understand. Choose between what, Dad?"
"You must choose between good and bad, between what is allowed and what is forbidden, between pleasant and nasty."
"And here?"
"Here it doesn't matter, there aren't any consequences. But in the future, there will be times when the consequences will be important and far-reaching. What you choose will make you who you are. Sometimes you'll choose well. Sometimes you won't. Sometimes you'll be able to ignore what you did and simply carry on like you did just now. That's what's called 'running away from responsibility'. You won't always be able to do that. Sometimes you'll have to stand up and face the consequences."
"So why did you let me carry on straight?"
"Because sometimes you can do that too," said the father. Then he continued. "Third rule: The starting point. That's the only thing you can't control. Everything else is in your hands. You can't always decide what events will occur in your life, but you'll always be able to choose how to respond to them. You can't choose the map, but you can choose the route.
Every choice adds to the large web of decisions you must make, the path in your life, the man you'll become."
"I've got a question", said the boy, pointing to the route he had taken. "Why did you say that this mat is my life, if it's only this part?"
"Your life really is the mat," answered the father. "Just this bit," and he pointed to the part that was not used. "This is the life you decided not to live."

בלק

Ground Meat

Meatballs with Peas
Mariuma

This is a favorite dish at Shanti House. If you like, it can be made with cooked fava beans (known locally as ful) rather than peas.
Serves 10

Meatballs
2 pounds (900 grams) ground beef
3½ ounces (100 grams) ground lamb fat
1 bunch parsley, chopped
1 tablespoon olive oil
1 tablespoon salt
1 egg
Canola oil, for frying

Sauce
2 tablespoons olive oil
3 onions, chopped
½ teaspoon sugar
7 cloves garlic, chopped
5 ounces (150 grams) tomato paste
1 tablespoon sweet paprika
1 teaspoon black pepper
1 heaping teaspoon turmeric
1 heaping teaspoon cumin
1 teaspoon salt
½ teaspoon hot paprika
2 cups (480 ml) water
Two 12-ounce (340 grams) packages frozen peas

Prepare meatballs: In a medium mixing bowl, combine beef, lamb fat, parsley, oil, salt, and egg. Wet hands and shape mixture into 1-inch balls. In a medium pan, heat oil over medium-high heat. Add meatballs and fry on all sides until golden. Transfer to a plate lined with paper towels to absorb excess oil.

Prepare sauce: In a large pot, heat oil over medium-high heat. Add onions, sugar, and garlic, and sauté for about 5 to 7 minutes, until brown. Add tomato paste, sweet paprika, pepper, turmeric, and cumin, and sauté for 1 minute. Stir in salt, hot paprika, and water, then add meatballs and peas. Bring to a boil, then reduce heat, cover pot, and simmer gently for about 1½ hours.

Tomatoes Stuffed with Ground Meat and Rice
Mariuma

Stuffed tomatoes are a delight to the eye and palate. This dish is perfect when lush round beefsteak tomatoes are in season.
Serves 10

10 large tomatoes

Filling
1 cup (200 grams) Persian white rice, rinsed
2 cups (480 ml) water
½ pound (225 grams) ground beef
Ground cumin
Ground coriander seeds
Salt and freshly ground black pepper
White pepper
Olive oil, for frying
1 cup chopped fresh parsley

Sauce
Vegetable oil, for frying
2 medium onions, chopped
1 teaspoon sugar
1 teaspoon turmeric
3½ ounces (100 grams) tomato paste
Salt and freshly ground black pepper
3 cups (720 ml) water

Using a sharp knife, cut tops off tomatoes. Carefully remove seeds and flesh, and reserve.

Prepare filling: In a medium pot, combine water and rice. Cover and bring to a boil over high heat, then reduce heat to low, and cook for about 8 minutes, until parboiled. Drain.

In a medium bowl, combine beef, cumin, coriander, salt, black pepper, and white pepper. Heat oil in a frying pan over medium-high heat, then add beef mixture and cook, stirring regularly, for about 5 minutes. Mix in rice and parsley.

Stuff tomato shells with beef mixture, and arrange in a large, wide-based pot so that they are close together.

Prepare sauce: Heat oil over medium-high heat. Add onions and sauté until golden. Stir in sugar, turmeric, tomato paste, salt, pepper, and water, and bring to a boil. Pour tomato sauce into pot with stuffed tomatoes, until tomatoes are covered. Bring to a boil over high heat, then cover, reduce heat, and cook for about 1 hour.

The Frog's Tale

One day, there was a frog race to see which frog could reach the top of a tall tower. Many people came to watch the race, though they didn't believe any frog could succeed.

Immediately after the race started, a few onlookers started shouting. "There's no point to this," they said. "These frogs will never make it."

Many frogs began to despair, but a few kept on climbing.

The crowd continued to shout discouraging remarks, with more people joining in. "What a waste of time," they shouted. "These frogs will never succeed."

Soon, all the frogs except one had dropped out of the race. One frog kept on climbing, despite everything. Eventually, that frog reached the top.

The other frogs looked at the victorious frog with amazement. "How did she do it?" they wondered.

One of the frogs approached the winning frog and asked, "How did you do it?"

There was no response. The question was repeated a few more times, until it became clear-the winning frog was deaf!

The moral of this story? Don't listen to people who put you down. Words are strong, so don't listen to ones that are discouraging.

If someone says you can't do something…pretend you are deaf, and do it anyway!

Ground Meat

Artichokes Filled with Ground Meat
Liat Turgeman, Head Girls' Instructor at Shanti House

This festive Moroccan dish is often served at Passover. For people who eat pulses on Passover, it's perfectly accompanied by steamed rice.
Serves 10

Artichokes
10 fresh artichoke hearts, or 1 pound (450 grams) frozen artichoke hearts
Salted water with lemon juice (for fresh artichokes), or salted water (for frozen artichokes)

Filling
1 pound (450 grams) ground beef
1 large onion, diced
2 eggs, beaten
1½ tablespoons matzah meal or breadcrumbs
¼ cup chopped parsley
Turmeric
Salt and ground black pepper
1 to 2 tablespoons water
2½ cups (250 grams) matzah meal or breadcrumbs
Canola oil, for frying

Roasting liquid
2 cups (480 ml) boiling water
1 tablespoon chicken soup powder
Salt and freshly ground black pepper
Turmeric
Juice from 1 lemon

Preheat oven to 350°F (180°C).

Prepare artichokes: For fresh artichokes: Peel and remove external leaves and hairy core. Heat a large pot of salted water with lemon juice until boiling. Add artichoke hearts and cook for 10 minutes. Drain and set aside. For frozen artichoke hearts: Heat a pot of salted water until boiling. Add artichoke hearts and blanch for a few minutes. Drain and set aside.

Prepare filling: In a medium bowl, combine ground beef, onion, 1 egg, matzah meal, parsley, turmeric, salt, and pepper. Place a mound of mixture on each artichoke heart, to form a ball in which the bottom is the artichoke and the top is the beef.

In a small bowl, combine remaining egg, water, turmeric, salt and pepper. Sprinkle matzah meal in a flat plate. Dredge stuffed artichoke hearts in egg mixture, then matzah meal to coat evenly. In a large frying pan, heat about 1 inch of oil over medium-high heat. Add stuffed artichoke hearts, and sauté on all sides until golden.

Prepare roasting liquid: In a deep baking pan, combine boiling water, soup powder, salt, pepper, and turmeric. Add artichoke hearts, and bake for 1 hour. Stir mixture occasionally, to coat artichokes that are not immersed in fluid. Bake until hearts are brown and cooking liquid thickens into a sauce.

Remove baking dish from oven, drizzle with lemon juice, and bake for another 5 minutes.

I Ate Lunch With G-d

A boy sat down on a park bench, opened his knapsack, and took out something to drink. The boy noticed an old man sitting on the same bench, and thought the man looked a little bit hungry. He took a piece of fruit out of his bag and offered it to the man.

The old man took the fruit thankfully, smiled at the child, and began to eat. The man's smile was so pleasant and wide, that the child decided he wanted to see it again. So when the man finished the fruit, the boy offered him a drink. Again, the stranger gave the boy a wide smile, his eyes shining happily, and took the drink. The child was delighted.

The boy and the old man sat, side by side, for the entire afternoon. They ate and drank together, smiling often but never saying a word. When it started getting dark, the boy decided to go home. When he got there, his mother noticed a look of peaceful happiness on his face.

"What happened at the park?" she asked. "You look really happy!"
"I had lunch with G-d," the boy replied. "And you know what? He has the biggest smile I've ever seen."

In the meantime, the old man also went home. He walked into his house, and saw that his son had come to visit. The son was surprised to see a look of happiness gleaming from the old man's face.
"What did you do today, Dad," he asked. "You look really happy."
"I had lunch with G-d," said the old man. "And you know what. He is much younger than I thought."

Don't underestimate the value of simple things like smiles, shared food, kind words, or attentive ears. These little things can change people's lives. Let the people that touch your life know how important they are to you. And don't be afraid to touch others so that you'll be important to them. In short, eat lunch with G-d.

Ground Meat

Meatballs in Artichoke, Fava Bean, and Sage Casserole
Meir Adoni, Catit

This recipe comes from a dish prepared by Meir's grandmother Mas'uda, who always wanted to inundate him with love, beans, and artichokes. Serve alongside steamed white rice.
Serves 10

Meatballs
1½ pounds (680 grams) ground turkey
1½ pounds (680 grams) ground veal neck
6 slices white bread, crusts removed, soaked in water and squeezed dry
2 eggs
2 teaspoons ground allspice
Salt and freshly ground black pepper
Vegetable oil, for frying

Casserole
½ cup (120 ml) extra-virgin olive oil
1 head garlic, divided into cloves and peeled
5 sage leaves
1 tablespoon coriander seeds
3 medium onions, finely diced
2 pounds (900 g) frozen artichoke hearts, diced
4 medium ripe tomatoes, grated
1 medium fennel, finely sliced

½ cup (120 ml) water
1 tablespoon chicken soup powder
1 pound (450 grams) frozen blanched fava beans, thawed and peeled
¼ cup (50 ml) freshly squeezed lemon juice
1 bunch fresh parsley, finely chopped
Salt and freshly ground black pepper

Prepare meatballs: In a medium bowl, combine turkey, veal, bread, eggs, allspice, salt, and pepper. Knead until combined, then refrigerate for at least 30 minutes (but no more than 24 hours). In a medium pan, heat some oil over medium-high heat. Shape a meatball and fry until brown on all sides. Taste and correct seasoning, if required.

Prepare casserole: In a wide pot, heat oil with 2 cloves garlic, sage, and coriander. Add onions, and sauté gently until transparent. Add artichoke hearts, tomatoes, and fennel. Cover and simmer for 15 minutes over low heat.

Mix in water and soup powder. Shape meat mixture into 1½-inch balls and gently arrange in a single layer on the base of the pan. Cover pan and cook for 10 minutes.

Add fava beans and lemon juice, and sprinkle parsley on top. Drizzle with a bit of olive oil before serving.

מסעי

Harvard and Stanford

This story is likely an urban legend, but has a powerful message.
A simply dressed woman and her husband, also dressed in a plain suit, arrived at the office of the president of Harvard University without an appointment. It was immediately obvious to the secretary that these poor, simple people had no business being at Harvard.
"We wish to see the president of the university," said the man softly.
"He is busy," said the secretary, without cracking a smile, and through clenched teeth. "He'll be busy all day."
"We'll wait till he is free," said the woman.
The secretary ignored them, hoping they would go away, but they didn't leave and her frustration grew until she finally decided to disturb the president.
"Perhaps if you come to talk to them for a few minutes, they will leave'" she said.
The university president sighed in annoyance, and came out towards the couple.
The woman spoke, "Our son studied here one year," she said. "He loved the place, and was very content here. About a year ago, he was killed in an accident. My husband and I would like to erect a memorial to him somewhere on campus."
The president was not moved by her words.
"Madam," he said irritably, "We cannot put a memorial to every person who studied here and dies. If we did, the place would look like a cemetery."
"Oh, no," said the woman, 'We weren't thinking of a statue. We thought we might donate a building."
The president rolled his eyes, and said condescendingly, 'Do you have any idea how much a building costs? We have just now invested $7.5 million in a new physics building. We don't have money to build another building"
The woman was quiet for a minute. The president was satisfied. Perhaps he would now be rid of the couple. And then the woman turned to her husband and said quite calmly:
"Is that what it costs to put up a university building? Then why don't we just erect our own university?"
Her husband nodded in silent agreement.
Mr. and Mrs. Stanford got up and left the office. They travelled back to Palo Alto, California, and founded a university there bearing their name. That university is the Stanford University, named after a son who attended Harvard, but whose parents were snubbed by a university president who was a bit too quick to judge others.

Ground Meat

Meatballs with Eggplant
Mariuma

This fragrant and satisfying casserole features meatballs, sliced eggplant, and dozens of garlic cloves.
Serves 10

Meatballs
2 pounds (900 grams) ground beef
3½ ounces (100 grams) ground lamb fat
1 bunch fresh parsley, chopped
1 tablespoon olive oil
1 tablespoon salt
1 large egg
Canola oil, for frying

Eggplant and garlic
Kosher salt
Hot water
4 medium eggplants, sliced lengthwise into 2-inch slices
Canola oil, for frying
2 heads garlic, cut widthwise and separated into cloves

Sauce
1 tablespoon extra-virgin olive oil
5 cloves garlic, crushed
¼ cup (60 ml) tomato paste
1 teaspoon sugar
Sweet paprika
Hot paprika
Ground cumin
Ground coriander seeds
Salt and freshly ground black pepper
2 cups (480 ml) water

Prepare meatballs: In a medium bowl, combine beef, lamb fat, parsley, oil, salt, and egg. Wet hands and shape mixture into 1-inch balls. In a medium pan, heat oil over medium-high heat. Add meatballs and fry on all sides until golden. Transfer to a plate lined with paper towels to absorb excess oil.

Prepare eggplant and garlic: In a medium bowl, dilute salt in hot water. Add eggplant slices, and let soak for several minutes. Remove eggplant, drain, and pat dry.
In a large frying pan, heat oil over medium high heat. Add eggplant slices, and fry until golden. Transfer to a plate lined with paper towels.
In a wide-based pot, arrange layers of eggplant and meatballs. Distribute garlic cloves between layers.

Prepare sauce: In a frying pan, heat oil over medium-high heat. Add garlic and sauté until golden. Stir in tomato paste, sugar, paprikas, cumin, coriander, salt, and pepper. Add water and bring to a boil. Pour sauce into pot with eggplant and meatballs, and bring to a boil. Cover, reduce heat to low, and simmer for 1 hour.

דברים

Only a Smile

She walked down the road on her way to the grocery store to buy some cheese, milk and eggs. In the middle of the road she saw a stranger who seemed sad, and smiled at him. She thought the smile might make him feel better. He, in turn, was reminded of the kindness of a friend who had offered him aid in the past, so when he got home, he wrote his old friend a letter of gratitude.

The friend received the letter a few days later, and was so delighted by it, that he left a big tip at a restaurant after eating a meal.

The waitress, surprised and overjoyed by the tip, gave part of it to a beggar on the street.

The beggar was infinitely grateful. He hadn't eaten in two days, and was cold, lonely, and hungry.

After he finished eating the meal he had purchased with the money he got from the waitress, he walked with a full belly to his dark and dirty room.

On his way, he found an abandoned, miserable looking puppy.

He brought the puppy home with him to warm up. The puppy was thankful to spend a night indoors rather than outside in the cold rain.

That night, a fire broke out in the beggar's room. It was a fierce fire, and quickly set the entire building alight. The puppy started barking soon after the fire started. He woke all the tenants, who made their way out of the building, and were saved from harm.

One of the tenants of the building was the anonymous young woman who had smiled at a stranger one day, with a look of warmth and sympathy that had cost her nothing. That smile ultimately helped save many people.

This is how the world turns. Whatever you send eventually returns to you. We are all connected, and everything is one.

If you are looking for love, you must first be a loving person. If no one smiles at you, you can be the one to smile.

No one is needier of a smile than the one who doesn't smile.

Ground Meat

Grape Leaf Cake, with Meat, Rice, Raisins, and Pistachios
Zachi Bukshester, Black & Burger

This dish gives diners an attractive and aromatic Israeli experience. Seal the pot tightly for perfectly steamed rice.
Serves 10

Oil, for greasing
½ pound (225 grams) fresh or preserved grape leaves, rinsed
½ pound (225 grams) Basmati rice, soaked in water for 1 hour and strained
½ cup (120 ml) extra-virgin olive oil
2 medium onions, coarsely diced
½ cup (1¾ ounces) (50 grams) pine nuts
½ cup (1¾ ounces) (50 grams) pistachios, shelled and toasted
1¾ ounces (50 grams) currants
½ pound (225 grams) ground beef
½ cup (120 ml) freshly squeezed lemon juice
¼ cup chopped fresh mint leaves
¼ cup chopped fresh parsley leaves
1 tablespoon baharat (Middle East spice mixture)
1 teaspoon salt
¼ cup (60 ml) water

Grease an 8-inch round pot, then line with 3 to 4 layers of grape leaves, so that the dark sides of the leaves face the sides of the pot, and the light sides face the center. Allow some leaves to extend beyond the top edge of the pot. These are used later, to cover the casserole.

In a wide pan, heat oil over medium-high heat. Add onions, pine nuts, and pistachios, and cook until onions are transparent and pine nuts are golden. Stir in rice and currants until combined. Mix in meat, stirring to ensure mixture stays crumbly. Add lemon juice, mint, parsley, baharat, and salt, then remove from heat.

Fill grape leaf-lined pot with beef mixture, and press mixture in lightly. Pour in water, then cover with a layer of grape leaves. Fold grape leaves extending around edge of pot over top, then cover with parchment paper. Place a small, oven-safe plate on top as a weight, then wrap with aluminum foil, and cover with a lid. Cook over low heat for 1½ hours.

To serve, invert pot over a serving dish, and let mixture slide out. Serve hot or at room temperature.

ואתחנן

The Farm

A mouse, peeking from its hole, saw a farmer and his wife open a parcel. 'I wonder what kind of food is in the parcel…,' thought the mouse in anticipation. To his shock and dismay, however, he saw the couple take a mousetrap out of the box.

The mouse ran into the yard, screaming, "There's a mousetrap in the house! There's a mousetrap in the house!"

The hen raised its head slowly, looked at the mouse, and cackled, "Mr. Mouse, I know this is a disaster from your point of view, but it is totally meaningless for me."

The mouse ran to the pig and exclaimed, "There's a mousetrap in the house! There's a mousetrap in the house!"

The pig showed a bit more compassion than the hen, and said, "I'm so sorry, Mr. Mouse, but there is nothing I can do except pray for your safety."

The mouse ran to the cow, and shouted, "There's a mousetrap in the house! There's a mousetrap in the house!"

The cow blinked once, then said, "A mousetrap. Really. As though I care. As though it could endanger me."

Feeling sad, frightened, and alone, the mouse returned to the house, understanding that he would be left to deal with the mousetrap all by himself.

In the middle of the night, a snapping sound, like the one made by an activated mousetrap, was heard.

The farmer's wife jumped out of her bed to see what was caught in the trap. In the dark she couldn't see that a venomous snake had been caught in the trap, not a mouse. The snake bit the woman angrily, and the woman screamed in agony, and fainted.

Her husband awoke, found her on the floor, and quickly rushed her to the hospital.

Doctors at the hospital did the best they could, then sent the woman home, albeit with a high fever, to recuperate.

Now, everyone knows the best treatment for a high fever is chicken soup. So the farmer took his axe, killed the chicken, and prepared fresh soup for his wife.

Friends and neighbors came to visit the sick woman, and sat by her bedside for several days. With all these people in the house, the farmer needed lots of food, so he killed the pig in order to feed the guests.

The chicken soup was good, but it didn't save the woman's life, and after a few days, she passed away. Hundreds of people came to the funeral. With all these people in the house, the farmer needed even more food. So he killed the cow.

The next time you hear about a problem you think does not concern you, remember that when the weakest member of a group is threatened, everyone is in danger.

Ground Meat

Mafrum
Gil Hovav, Author and Publisher

These stuffed vegetables are surprisingly easy to make. Delicious served on rice or couscous.

Serves 10

Vegetables
6 potatoes, peeled
6 large carrots, peeled
1¼ pounds (570 grams) ground beef
2 thick bread slices, soaked in water, squeezed dry, and grated
8 cloves garlic, chopped
2 handfuls fresh dill, chopped
Pinch of cinnamon
Salt and freshly ground black pepper
2 eggs, beaten
2 tablespoons ketchup
Vegetable oil, for frying

Sauce
1½ 28-ounce (800 grams) cans of crushed tomatoes
3½ ounces (100 grams) tomato paste
1 tablespoon chicken soup powder
1 tablespoon ground caraway
1 cup boiling water

Prepare vegetables: Slice potatoes and carrots lengthwise into 1-inch thick slices. Make a lengthwise slit along the center of each slice, so that it can be opened like a pocket. Leave ends intact, so that vegetables don't break when stuffed.

In a medium bowl, combine beef, bread, garlic, dill, cinnamon, salt, and pepper. Gently stuff filling into vegetables.

In a separate bowl, beat eggs with ketchup until combined.

Heat about 2 inches of oil in a frying pan over medium-high heat. Dip each stuffed vegetable in egg mixture, then fry for about 2 to 3 minutes on each side, until golden. Transfer to a plate lined with paper towels to absorb excess oil.

Prepare sauce: In same pan, combine tomatoes, tomato paste, soup powder, caraway, and water, and bring to a boil over medium-high heat. Gently add stuffed vegetables, and bring to a boil again. Reduce heat to medium, cover, and cook for about 40 minutes, until vegetables and meat are cooked through. Serve hot.

עקב

Our True Worth

In a room with about 200 auditors, a well-known lecturer began his lecture by holding up a $20 bill and asking, "Which one of you is interested in this bill?"

People began to raise their hands.

"I'm about to give this bill to one of you," he said, "but first let me do this…" and he began crumpling the bill.

"Who is still interested in the bill?" he asked.

The same hands were up in the air.

"Good," he continued, "and what if I do this?"

He threw the bill on the floor and started crushing it with the sole of his shoe. Then he lifted the crushed, wrinkled dirty bill and asked again, "Now, who is interested in it?"

Just as many hands were raised again.

"My friends, you have just learned a very important lesson. It didn't matter what I did to the bill, you still wanted it because its value didn't decline. It was still worth $20. Many times in our lives, we feel bent, crumpled or stomped on, as a result of bad decisions we have made or unfavorable circumstances we encountered. We may feel worthless, but we're not. It does not matter what happened, or what will happen. Your worth never declines.

You are special. Never forget that! Don't let yesterday's disappointments obscure tomorrow's dreams."

Desserts

Desserts

Baked Apples in Crispy Coating
Aner Zalel, Dallal Bakery

Baked apples are always a treat. In honor of Shabbat, we decided to upgrade simple baked apples by dressing them in a crumbly coating and stuffing them with a sweet, nutty filling.
Serves 10

Apples
10 green apples, peeled and cored
2 tablespoons ground cinnamon
¼ teaspoon ground cloves
¼ teaspoon ground nutmeg
¼ teaspoon ground allspice
6 tablespoon currants
¼ cup (1 ounce) (30 grams) chopped pistachios
7 dried apricots, chopped
Brown sugar
5 teaspoons margarine, soft

Streusel
2 sticks (9 ounces) (250 grams) margarine, cold
2 cups (200 grams) blanched almonds (or mixture of peeled nuts)
1¾ cups (240 grams) all-purpose flour
1¼ cups (250 grams) sugar
1 teaspoon ground cinnamon

Prepare apples: Hollow out apples, leaving about ½ inch of flesh on sides and bottom.
In a medium bowl, combine cinnamon, cloves, nutmeg, allspice, currants, pistachios, and apricots. Stuff each apple until a mound forms on the top, then place about ½ teaspoon of margarine on each mound.
Preheat oven to 350°F (175°C), and lightly grease a baking sheet.
Prepare streusel: Place margarine, almonds, flour, sugar, and cinnamon in a food processor, and pulse just until crumby. Using your hands, press streusel all over each apple to make a crumbly coating.
Arrange apples in baking dish, and bake for about 45 minutes, until streusel is crispy and golden. If crumbs begin to burn during baking, lower temperature to 300°F (150°C). Serve warm

A Lesson in Modesty

It was around noon when I had finished some errands in town and was walking home. I walked along Main Street, enjoying the warm, end-of-spring sun until I reached my bus stop. I sat on the bench and watched the other people waiting for the bus. There was a woman with overflowing baskets of food who looked like she was returning from her weekly shopping trip; a middle-aged couple holding hands, a young woman with a baby stroller, and two teenagers. Like me, all of them were waiting for the bus.
Two minutes after I sat down on the bench, a young woman arrived at the stop. I won't describe her now. Let it suffice to say that modesty was not her outstanding quality. In other words, more of her was naked than dressed. She also stood at the bus stop, waiting for the bus.
I took a newspaper out of my bag and started reading it, when out of the corner of my eye I saw a figure dressed in black approaching. As the figure approached, I noticed it was a religious-looking man, with a big black beard, a long black coat, and a black hat. The man glanced at the people waiting at the stop, then noticed the young woman. He lowered his gaze, and stepped back a couple of steps. Then, he walked behind the bus stop and went into the green grocer's shop.
"He probably prefers waiting for the bus there than being tempted by the immodest girl," I thought to myself.
But to my surprise, he came out of the shop a few minutes later holding a big, red, shiny apple. He returned to the station, and of all the people standing there walked straight to the young woman. He offered her the apple saying, "Take it, it's for you."
The young woman was very surprised, not understanding what he wanted. "For me?" she asked with amazement, "Why?" she said, voicing the question mark in the minds of all the people present in the station and listening intently to the ongoing dialogue.
The man raised his head, looked her straight in the eyes and said with a smile, "Eve, too, didn't know she was naked until she ate from the apple...."

ראה

123

 Desserts

Cinnamon Buns
Uri Scheft, Lehamim Bakery

This delicious recipe fills the kitchen with an irresistible aroma, reminding everyone in the house of life's simpler pleasures.
Makes about 25 3-inch rolls

Dough
¾ cup + 1 tablespoon (200 ml) lukewarm water
1 ounce (30 grams) fresh yeast
5⅗ cups (700 grams) all-purpose white flour
2 eggs
½ cup (100 grams) sugar
½ teaspoon salt
1 stick (4½ ounces) (125 grams) margarine, room temperature

Filling
½ stick (2½ ounces) (65 grams) margarine, soft
¼ cup (50 grams) sugar
2 tablespoons cinnamon

Syrup
¼ cup (60 ml) water
¼ cup (50 grams) sugar

Prepare dough: Arrange all of the ingredients in small bowls on your work surface.

Pour water into a medium bowl, add yeast, and stir until the yeast dissolves. Add flour, eggs, sugar, salt, and margarine. Knead with your hands for about 10 minutes, until dough is soft but elastic (flexible). Shape dough into a ball, cover with a clean kitchen cloth, and set aside to rise for about 1 hour, until dough doubles in size. Line a baking sheet with parchment paper.

Punch down dough to remove air, and divide into two even parts. Roll out each part into a 15 x 8-inch rectangle that is about ¼ inch thick.

Prepare filling: Spread margarine evenly on each rectangle, then sprinkle with sugar and cinnamon. Roll rectangles into a log, and pinch edges to seal. Slice each log into about eight 1½-inch pieces. Arrange slices on lined baking sheet, and set aside to rise for 45 minutes, or until dough almost doubles in size.

Preheat oven to 375°F (190°C). Bake rolls for about 12 minutes, until golden.

Prepare syrup: In the meantime, in a small pot, bring water and sugar to a boil over medium-high heat. Cook for 3 to 4 minutes, until a syrup forms. Brush warm cinnamon buns with hot syrup, and serve.

The Cookie Bag

At a busy airport one night, a woman realized she had arrived far too early for her flight. She bought herself a good book at the bookshop, a bag of cookies at the snack bar, and looked for a place to sit while she waited for her flight. She soon found a bench in a quiet corner of the airport, and sat down to read.

The woman was so engrossed in her book that she didn't notice a man sit down next to her. In fact, she wouldn't have noticed him at all except for the fact that he stretched his hand into the bag of cookies resting between them on the bench. He took one cookie after another, as if they belonged to him. The woman decided to ignore the man's rudeness, thinking that if she decided not to create a fuss, perhaps he would go away.

The woman continued reading her book, though she found it a bit hard to concentrate now. The audacious man kept taking cookies from the bag, so she started taking them too. For every one cookie he took, she took one herself. 'I wouldn't be surprised if he asks me to buy him some coffee soon too,' she thought to herself.

When there was just one cookie left, the woman wondered what he would do. With a bashful smile, the man picked up the last cookie, and broke it in half. He put one half in his mouth, and offered her the other.

Annoyed, the woman took the cookie half in her hand, and she thought to herself, 'Not only is he a thief, but he is also rude. He didn't even thank me!'

A few minutes after the cookies were finished, the woman's flight was announced. She put her book into her purse, got up, and walked away. She walked faster than usual, in fact, eager to put distance between her and the rude cookie thief.

A few minutes later, the woman had boarded the plane and found her seat. She settled in, then rummaged in her purse to find her book. Instead of her book, however, she found a full bag of cookies.

Shocked and surprised, she suddenly understood what had happened. The cookies the man had been eating were HIS. She had been the cookie thief, not him! Not only that, but he had shared them with her without a word, and she hadn't even said 'Thank you'. Not only that, but she had been incredibly rude. She was, in fact, the rude cookie thief.

How many times in our lives are we are positive that we know something absolutely, and only later, sometimes too late, we discover that what we believed, or what we thought was the truth, was not actually so.

Keep an open heart and an open mind, and don't forget to ask yourself whether you might be eating someone else's cookies.

Desserts

Date Cookies
Tzvia Azulai, Food Writer at Chef and La'isha magazines

Achieve the beloved flavor of maamoul (Middle Eastern filled cookies) without the effort of filling each individual cookie.
Makes 50 biscuits

Dough
7 cups (about 1 kg) white flour
2 teaspoons (10 grams) baking powder
1¾ sticks (7 ounces) (200 grams) margarine, soft
1 cup (240 ml) orange juice
2 tablespoons rose water, or one teaspoon rose water extract
1 cup (240 ml) canola oil
¾ cup (150 grams) sugar
¼ teaspoon salt

Filling
1 pound (450 grams) pitted dates
1 pound (450 grams) date spread
10½ ounces (300 grams) chopped walnuts
7 ounces (200 grams) raisins
2 tablespoons ground cinnamon
¼ cup brown sugar

Powdered sugar, for sprinkling

Preheat oven to 325°F (165°C) and line a baking sheet with parchment paper.
Prepare dough: In the bowl of a food processor, combine flour, baking powder, margarine, orange juice, rose water, oil, sugar and salt. Process just until a soft dough forms.
Divide dough into 8 equal parts, and roll out each part into a 12 x 4-inch rectangle that is about ½ inch thick.
Prepare filling: In a medium bowl, combine dates with date spread until smooth. Spread mixture evenly on dough rectangles, then sprinkle with walnuts, raisins, sugar, and cinnamon.
Fold bottom third of each rectangle upwards, to cover middle.
Fold top third of each rectangle downwards, to cover middle. Each rectangle now has three layers of dough, sandwiching two layers of filling.
Slice each layered rectangle into several 1-inch wide cookies, taking care not to slice all the way through the cookies. Transfer to baking sheet and bake for about 25 minutes, until golden.
Remove cookies from the oven, and slice through to the bottom, to separate each cookie. Transfer to a wire rack to cool, then sprinkle with powdered sugar. May be stored in an airtight container for up to 2 weeks.

Coconut Malabi
Tzvia Azulai, Food Writer at Chef and La'isha magazines

This non-dairy dessert has a creamy texture and refreshing coconut flavor.
Makes 12 individual servings

Malabi
1 14-ounce (400 grams) can condensed coconut milk
1¾ cups (400 ml) water
¾ cup (150 grams) sugar
2 packages (½ ounce) (14 grams) gelatin
1 tablespoon boiling water

כי תצא

3 tablespoons corn flour
¼ cup (60 ml) cold water
1 teaspoon coconut extract

Syrup
1 cup (200 grams) sugar
1 cup (240 ml) water
1 teaspoon coconut extract or rose water
Drop of preservative-free red food coloring
Sliced pistachios, for garnish

Prepare malabi: In a small pot, combine coconut milk, water, and sugar, and bring to a boil over medium-high heat.
In a small cup, dissolve gelatin in boiling water, then add to pot. In a small cup, dissolve corn flour in cold water, then gradually add to pot, stirring constantly to avoid lumps.
Bring mixture just to boil, then remove from heat, and mix in coconut extract. Let cool slightly, then distribute evenly among individual serving dishes. Cover with plastic wrap, and refrigerate until cool. May be kept for up to 3 days.
Prepare syrup: In a small pot, combine sugar, water, coconut extract, and food coloring, and bring to a boil over medium-high heat.
Cook at a boil for another 5 to 7 minutes, until a thick syrup forms. Remove from heat and cool, then refrigerate until ready to serve. To serve, pour chilled syrup over chilled malabi, and sprinkle with pistachios.

Experience

A farmer's donkey fell into an old dry well, and began braying for help. As the donkey was already old and the well was dry, the farmer decided to bury the donkey in the well, and plug the well at the same time.
The farmer summoned all his neighbors who came with their shovels and started throwing dirt into the well. In the beginning the donkey brayed, but after a few minutes he grew quiet. The farmers continued shoveling dirt into the well and the donkey remained quiet.
The farmer came by a few minutes later and peered into the well. To his amazement, he saw the donkey standing on its four legs! Each time a shovel of dirt was thrown into the well, the donkey just shook the dirt off his back, and stepped onto the dirt. Thus the dirt collected at the bottom of the well, and with each additional shovelful, the donkey rose a few inches higher. Soon the well was filled, and the donkey walked out.
What's the moral of the story? When dirt is thrown at you (even by the people who are closest to you), crying and whining won't help. Just shake off the dirt, step on it, and move on!

Desserts

Puff Pastry Baklava
Ora Ben Yosef, Former Shanti House Housemother

The youth at Shanti House call Ora 'Grandma' and in exchange, she cooks Grandma-style food for them, filled with love and flavor. Her baklava is an excellent example of food that sweetens the mouth, and the heart.

Makes about 25 pieces

Baklava
2 sheets (18 ounces) (510 grams) puff pastry, frozen and thawed
½ pound (225 grams) unsalted peanuts or pistachios, toasted
1 tablespoon cinnamon
2 tablespoons sugar
1 tablespoon rose water

Syrup
2 cups (400 grams) sugar
1½ cups + 3 tablespoons (400 ml) water
Juice and zest from 1 lemon
2 tablespoons rose water
Whole peanuts or pistachios, for garnish

Prepare baklava: Preheat oven to 400°F (200°C). Divide puff pastry in half. Roll out one half into a 10 x 12-inch rectangle, and press into a baking pan.

In a food processor, combine peanuts, cinnamon, sugar, and rose water. Pulse just until peanuts are coarsely ground, and mixture is combined.

Spread peanut mixture evenly in pan. Roll out remaining puff pastry into a 10 x 12-inch rectangle and place on top. Using a sharp knife, cut diagonal lines across surface of pastry, to make a diamond pattern. Bake for 30 minutes, until golden

Prepare syrup: While baklava is baking, combine sugar, water, lemon juice, and lemon zest in a small pot. Bring to a boil over medium-high heat, then reduce heat to medium, and gently boil for about 20 minutes. Remove syrup from heat, and mix in rose water. Pour hot syrup over hot baklava, and let sit for 30 minutes before serving, until baklava cools. Garnish with peanuts.

כי תבוא

G-d's Coffee

At a meeting in the home of an old professor, a group of well-established university graduates complained about the stress of work and life in general. The professor went into his kitchen to prepare coffee, and returned carrying a tray loaded with all kinds of mugs: china, plastic, glass, and crystal. Some of the mugs looked very plain, while others looked expensive. He asked his guests to select their own mugs, and pour themselves coffee.

When all the guests were sitting with mugs of coffee in their hands, the professor spoke.

"I wonder whether you have noticed," he said, "that you have all taken expensive-looking mugs, and none of you have taken simple, cheap-looking ones. It's very natural to want nothing but the best for oneself, but maybe that is the source of your problems and stress. Rest assured that the cup does not improve the quality of the coffee. In some cases, the cup can even obscure what you are drinking. You all just wanted some coffee, but all of you consciously chose the fanciest cups. Some of you even looked at other people's cups before selecting your own cups.

Think of it like this: Life is the coffee; work, money, status: these are the cups. However, they are only the vessels we use to hold and contain life. The type of cup we use doesn't define or change the quality of life we live."

It is the coffee that G-d makes, not the cup. Sometimes, because we are so busy focusing on the cup, we don't succeed in enjoying the coffee. The happiest people in the world aren't those who have the best of everything. They are those who extract the best out of everything."

Live simply, love generously, be caring, speak gently, and leave the rest to G-d.

Desserts

Daniel's Chocolate Cake
Ben Ami Bertini Shavit, Café Ben Ami

Ben Ami has been donating cakes and pastries to Shanti House for many years, and this is a wonderful opportunity to thank him again. Ben Ami invented this flourless cake recipe for his son Daniel, who suffers from Celiac. This recipe is also suitable for Passover.

Makes one 10-inch round or 13 x 11-inch cake

1¾ sticks (7 ounces) (200 grams) margarine
1 cup (200 grams) sugar
7 ounces (200 grams) bittersweet chocolate, melted
5 eggs
5 tablespoons potato flour
½ teaspoon baking powder
Chopped walnuts or hazelnuts, optional

Preheat oven to 350°F (180°C), and lightly grease a 10-inch round or 13 x 11-inch baking dish.
In a medium bowl, mix margarine and sugar until creamy. Mix in melted chocolate until combined. Gradually add eggs, one at a time, mixing well after each addition.
Sift in potato flour and baking powder, mixing just until batter is smooth.
Pour into baking pan, and sprinkle nuts on top, if you like. Bake for about 20 minutes, or until a toothpick inserted in the center comes out moist, but not wet.

Semolina Cake
Dana Livnat-Gazit, Volunteer at Shanti House

Rich in flavor and aroma, this cake has a marvelous texture, and leaves a satisfied feeling in the stomach.
Makes one 12 x 8-inch cake

Cake
1 cup (240 ml) vegetable oil, plus more for greasing
1 cup (200 grams) semolina
1 cup (200 grams) sugar
1 cup (100 grams) desiccated coconut
1 cup (100 grams) coarsely chopped walnuts
2 teaspoons (10 grams) baking powder
2 teaspoons (10 grams) vanilla sugar
¾ cup (190 ml) freshly squeezed orange juice with pulp

Syrup
2 cups (480 ml) water
1 cup (200 grams) sugar
A few drops of rose water

Preheat oven to 350°F (180°C), and grease a 12 x 8-inch baking pan.
Prepare cake: In a large mixing bowl, combine semolina, sugar, coconut, walnuts, baking powder, vanilla sugar, orange juice, and oil. Transfer batter to baking pan, and bake for 40 minutes, or until a toothpick inserted into the center comes out dry with crumbs.
Prepare syrup: While cake is baking, combine water and sugar in a small pot, and bring to a boil over medium-high heat. Continue boiling mixture until a syrup forms. Remove from heat, add rose water, and set aside to cool. Pour cooled syrup on hot cake.

The Experiment (A True Story)

A teacher in Ireland asked her students to bring a plastic bag and a bag of potatoes the next day to school. The students did as they were told, and the teacher gave them the following assignment: Choose a potato for each person in your life whom you have not forgiven for something they had done to you.
The students selected potatoes from their bags and wrote on each one the name of the person, as well as the date of the episode for which they had not forgiven them. Then they put the potatoes in the plastic bag. Some of the students had bags that were very heavy indeed.
The teacher instructed the students to carry the bags with the potatoes around for a whole week, wherever they went—to school, to extracurricular activities, to the playground, even to bed at night.
The nuisance of carrying the bags around during the week clearly demonstrated to the students how heavy this weight could be, and how they needed to be very careful not to forget it anywhere.
Quite naturally, and as can happen to vegetables that are banged too much, the contents of the bag soon became moldy, sticky, and putrid.
Grudges are like these potatoes. Toting them around with us everywhere is the price we pay for withholding forgiveness and holding on to pain and anger.
Sometimes, we think forgiveness is a gift we give people. In fact, it is a gift we give to ourselves.

Desserts

Walnut Carrot Cake
Micky Shemo, Shemo Bakery

Baked on Thursday, this aromatic cake will stay fragrant and moist throughout Shabbat. This cake is dairy free, as it calls for oil rather than butter. Replace the carrots with squash, if you like.

Makes one 12 x 4-inch loaf

¾ cup (180 ml) canola oil
1 cup (200 grams) sugar
1⅓ cups (180 grams) all-purpose flour
½ teaspoon baking powder
¼ teaspoon baking soda
1 teaspoon ground cinnamon
¼ teaspoon ground ginger
¼ teaspoon ground nutmeg
2 large eggs
3 large carrots (⅔ pounds) (300 grams), peeled and finely grated
½ cup (50 grams) coarsely chopped walnuts

Preheat oven to 330°F (165°C). Line a 12 x 4-inch loaf pan with parchment paper.
In the bowl of an electric mixer, combine oil and sugar at high speed until smooth.
Add flour, baking powder, baking soda, cinnamon, ginger, and nutmeg. Mix at low speed for about 30 seconds.
Add eggs, carrots, and walnuts, stirring just until ingredients are combined.
Pour mixture into loaf pan, and bake for about 45 minutes, or until a toothpick inserted into the center comes out with moist crumbs.

Quince Jam
Yechiel & Ronen Philosoph, Balkan Catering

This jam is perfect for serving at Rosh Hashanah, when quince is in season. It is delicious spread on fresh challah or toast, or as a filling for croissants.

Makes about 2 pounds

Water, with a few drops of lemon juice
2 pounds (900 grams) fresh quince, rinsed and peeled
4 cups (800 grams) sugar
Juice from 2 lemons
6 cloves
5 ounces (150 grams) chopped walnuts, recommended

Place water with lemon juice into a large bowl. Coarsely grate quince into bowl. (Lemon-infused water keeps quince from browning).
In a heavy-based pot, combine sugar, lemon juice, cloves, and walnuts. Strain quince, and add to pot. Bring mixture to a boil over medium-high heat, stirring regularly with a wooden spoon. Reduce heat to low, and simmer for about 30 minutes, stirring occasionally, until a thick jam forms.
To check for readiness, drop a bit of jam onto a plate, and let sit for 30 seconds. If jam stabilizes and crystallizes, it's ready.
Remove jam from heat and let cool completely. Transfer to a sterilized jar and refrigerate for up to 6 months.

Wine Vinegar

A group of archaeologists was conducting a dig in an isolated area close to an old estate when to their surprise they uncovered a small, sealed wooden barrel. After cleaning the outside of the barrel, an engraved inscription became visible. The inscription dated to 995, and stated that the wine in the barrel was from the excellent grape harvest of 815.

One of the archaeologists, realizing he had a treasure in his hands, carefully took the barrel into town to be examined by expert vintners. The vintners' examination revealed that this was the oldest wine barrel in the world, and likely contained superb wine that was worth a fortune.

Rumor spread quickly, and interest in the barrel grew. The company that owned the rare find decided to sell the barrel at a public auction. The auction was attended by wealthy people and wine lovers from all over the world, and everyone hoped to be able to buy the wine. The opening price was high, but this didn't deter anyone, and the bidding was fierce. Eventually, the barrel was sold to an elderly French billionaire who was an avid antique collector and wine lover.

The Frenchman was ecstatic. In his mind's eye, he saw himself bringing the rare object home, keeping it amongst the rare antiques in his collection, knowing that its price would increase as time went by. The man lifted the barrel in front of the crowd and bowed. Suddenly, perhaps due to the barrel's weight, the man lost his grip on the barrel, and it fell out of his hands crashing to the ground. Its contents began pouring out. Quick-thinking members of the audience rushed out cups, mugs, and glasses, hoping to collect some of the precious liquid before it would be lost forever. They tasted the wine cautiously. Then each of them in turn made a terrible face. The wine was sour, repellent, downright nauseating! If the barrel had not fallen, the man would have kept the wine behind armored glass in his antique room.

His grandson would have inherited the treasure, offered it at another auction, and earned a fortune. The barrel would have been kept behind the glass of another antique lover, and so on, and so on. Nobody would ever have known that the expensive choice wine was sour wine.

Desserts

Raybe Biscuits
Hadar Yiftah-Tutya, Matamey Gourmet

Raybe means sand in Arabic, and it is the sandy texture of these cookies that makes them so delicious. Jews of North African descent traditionally prepare these cookies for very festive occasions.

Makes about 20 biscuits

1½ cups (200 grams) all-purpose flour
⅘ stick (3½ ounces) (100 grams) margarine
¼ cup (60 ml) vegetable oil
½ cup (60 grams) powdered sugar
2 teaspoons (10 grams) vanilla sugar
Zest from 1 lemon, or 1 teaspoon rose water essence

Raw peanuts, blanched almonds, or pistachios, for garnish
Powdered sugar, for sprinkling

In the bowl of a food processor, combine flour, margarine, oil, sugars, and lemon zest. Pulse just until a dough forms. Shape dough into a ball, wrap in plastic wrap, and chill for at least 30 minutes. Preheat oven to 350°F (180°C), and line a baking sheet with parchment paper.
Roll dough into ½-inch balls, and press a few nuts in the center of each ball. Arrange cookies on a lined baking sheet, leaving a 1-inch space between cookies to allow them to spread during baking. Bake for 10 to 12 minutes, until biscuits stabilize a bit, and are golden around the edges. Be careful not to overbake. Remove from oven, transfer to a wire cooling rack, and let cool until completely stable.

Halva Squares
Barry Sayag, Tatti Bread

These biscuits are made from thin layers of almond shortbread pastry and halva, which is made from tahini. Delicate and delightful.

Makes about 35 biscuits

1¾ cups (190 grams) powdered sugar, plus more for sprinkling
3½ sticks (14 ounces) (400 grams) margarine, cold and cut into small cubes
1 teaspoon pure vanilla extract
Pinch of salt
4 cups (500 grams) flour
1½ ounces (50 grams) ground almonds
1 large egg
1 large egg yolk
11 ounces (300 grams) halva

In the bowl of a food processor, or an electric mixer fitted with the hook attachment, combine the icing sugar, margarine, vanilla, flour, almonds, and salt. Process until crumbly. Add egg and egg white, and process until dough forms.
Roll into a ball, wrap in plastic cling wrap, and refrigerate for at least 30 minutes. Line a baking sheet with parchment paper.
Divide chilled dough into 3 even parts. On a lightly floured surface, thinly roll out each part into an 8 x 6-inch rectangle that is about ⅛-inch thick. Transfer dough to a baking sheet lined with parchment paper and chill for 30 minutes.

Preheat oven to 350°F (180°C). Pierce chilled dough leaves with a fork several times, then bake for 20 minutes, or until golden. Set aside to cool.

When dough cools, place halvah in a microwave-safe bowl, and heat gently until soft and spreadable.

Place one rectangular piece of crust on your work surface, and spread half of the halvah on top. Place another crust on top, then spread remaining halvah. Top with remaining rectangular crust, then press down gently, to bind.

Cut rectangle into ¾-inch squares, and sprinkle icing sugar before serving. May be stored in an airtight container at room temperature for up to 1 week.

A Glass of Milk

In a small town near a big city, there was a poor boy who paid for his schooling by selling items door to door. One day, the boy hadn't sold anything by noontime, and was very hungry. He hadn't even earned the 10 cents he needed to buy a meal.

He knocked on the door of a house, hoping to sell at least one item in order to have enough money to buy some food. A young woman opened the door, and the boy asked if she would like to buy one of the items he was selling.

The woman didn't want to buy anything, but she noticed that the boy looked rather hungry and, without asking, brought him a large glass of milk.

The boy drank it slowly, and then asked, "How much do I owe you?"

"You don't owe me a thing," she answered.

"Thank you," he said earnestly, "from the bottom of my heart."

When Howard Kelly left the house, he felt physically fortified, and his belief in people and in G-d was strengthened.

Years later, the woman who had answered the door that day became critically ill. Local doctors were unable to cure her, and they sent her to a hospital in the big city to consult with a specialist about her disease.

That specialist was Dr. Howard Kelly, and when he heard from which town the patient had come, his eyes lit up. He went into the patient's room, and recognized the woman immediately. At that moment, he determined to do his utmost to save her life.

The woman stayed in the hospital for several months, and eventually won the battle against the rare disease. The day the woman was supposed to check out of the hospital, Dr. Kelly had her bill be transferred to his office. He looked at it, wrote something in the margin, and sent the bill to her room.

The woman dreaded opening the bill. She was sure she would have to pay it for the rest of her life. When she finally opened it, she read the following words in the margin: "Paid in full by one glass of milk. Dr. Howard Kelly."

Tears of happiness ran down her face, and with a lightened heart, she prayed, "Thank you Lord for your love that has spread into these people's hearts and hands."

There is a proverb which says, "Cast thy bread on the water." The good deed which you do today may aid you or someone you love at the least expected moment. If you haven't been rewarded today for your good deed, at least you have made the world a better place. Isn't that the meaning of life?

Desserts

Masapan: Moroccan Marzipan
Ayelet Or, OM

These festive Moroccan biscuits are traditionally served to break the Yom Kippur fast.

Makes about 40 cookies

Water
1 pound (450 grams) raw whole almonds
2½ cups (500 grams) sugar
1 cup (240 ml) water
Powdered sugar, for dusting
Food coloring, optional
Walnut or pecan halves, optional

Bring a pot of water to a boil, then remove from heat. Add almonds and soak for about 1 minute. Pour almonds into a strainer, and rinse with cold water. Peel off skin with your fingers, then dry with a kitchen cloth.

Place almonds in the bowl of a food processor and grind with short pulses. Take care that almonds don't become heated during the pulsing process.

In a small pot, bring sugar and water to a boil over medium-high heat. Continue boiling for a couple of minutes, until a golden thick syrup forms.

Add ground almonds and cook over low heat, stirring constantly, for about 20 minutes, or until a soft, malleable dough forms. If dough is too sticky, stir in a bit of water.

Transfer almond dough to a mixing bowl, and let sit until cool enough to handle. Dust hands with powdered sugar to prevent dough from sticking, and shape dough into individual units.

If you like, tint with food coloring, then shape into small balls and sandwich between nut halves.

Yoyo: Fried Biscuits
Ayelet Or, OM

These festive Moroccan biscuits are traditionally served at the end of Yom Kippur to break the fast. They are suitable for any family festivity.

Makes about 40 biscuits

Dough
4 eggs
¼ cup (60 ml) vegetable oil
⅓ cup (80 ml) freshly squeezed orange juice
Grated zest from 1 orange
2 tablespoons sugar
4 cups (560 grams) all-purpose flour, plus more for dusting
Vegetable oil, for deep frying

Syrup
2 cups (400 grams) sugar
1 cup (240 ml) water
Juice from 1 lemon

1 cup (100 grams) desiccated coconut, for dipping

Prepare dough: In a large mixing bowl, combine eggs, oil, orange juice, orange zest, sugar, and flour until a slightly oily dough forms. On a lightly floured surface, roll out dough until it is about ⅜-inch thick. Cut rounds using a cup with a 2-inch diameter. Remove the center of each round using a cup with a 1½-inch diameter.

In a frying pan, heat 2 inches of oil over medium-high heat. Fry dough rings on both sides until golden, then transfer to a plate lined with paper towel. Let cool.

Prepare syrup: In a small pot, bring sugar, water, and lemon juice to a boil over medium-high heat. Reduce heat to medium and cook until a thick syrup forms. Remove from heat and cool slightly.

Dip cooled biscuits in warm syrup, then in coconut. For maximum crunchiness, serve shortly after baking.

The Love Box

Once, in a small town, lived a widower with his only daughter. They had barely enough money to live on, and certainly no luxuries. Just before Christmas, the man discovered that his young daughter had spent a lot of money on a roll of expensive golden paper. He was very angry when he saw that she had used the paper to wrap a wooden box as a Christmas gift.

The next day, the child brought the wrapped box as a gift for her father. The father regretted his anger, and opened the box. To his astonishment, he saw that it was empty.

He reprimanded his daughter sternly, "Don't you know, young lady, that one must put a gift into the box?"

With tears in her eyes, the child said to her father, "But daddy, there is a gift in the box. I filled it with kisses, a whole lot of sweet kisses, especially for you."

Again the father regretted his anger, and asked his daughter to forgive him.

Some time afterwards, the daughter fell ill with a fatal disease from which she didn't recover.

Left in his solitude, the man kept the golden box next to his bed to the end of his life. Every time he missed his beloved daughter, he opened the box and took out one of the imaginary kisses which his daughter, the girl who loved him so much, had put in.

Each and every one of us receives a golden box filled with love from those around us: our parents, siblings, and children, our friends and colleagues, from nature, Creation and G-d. No other possession in this world is as infinite and as valuable.

Ingredient Index

Apples
Baked Apples in Crispy Coating 122
Carrot and Kohlrabi Salad with Citrus Vinaigrette and Walnuts 22
Chicken in Apples, Cinnamon and Caramel Sauce 68

Artichokes
Artichokes Filled with Ground Meat 110
Chicken with Artichokes 64
Meatballs in Artichoke, Fava Bean, and Sage Casserole 112

Artichokes, Jerusalem
Chicken in Apples, Cinnamon and Caramel Sauce 68
Vegetables Stuffed with Meat, Rice, and Lentils 100

Basil
Asian Chreime on a Bed of Couscous 34
Chicken with Potatoes and Red Peppers (dried) 78
Tuscany Baked Fish 42

Beets
Raw Beet Salad 28
Vegetables Stuffed with Meat, Rice, and Lentils 100

Carrots
Apio: Root Vegetable Dish 29
Asian Chreime on a Bed of Couscous 34
Carrot and Kohlrabi Salad with Citrus Vinaigrette and Walnuts 22
Chicken in Coconut Sauce 78
Chicken Stew with Israeli Couscous and Vegetables 80
Chicken with String Beans 88
Chickpea Casserole with Ginger, Tomato, and Date Honey 30
Cooked Olive Salad 24
Mafrum 118
Meatlovers Meat Sauce 106
Pal'u–Bukharin Rice Dish 70
Walnut Carrot Cake 132

Celery
Apio: Root Vegetable Dish 29
Asian Chreime on a Bed of Couscous 34
Carrot and Kohlrabi Salad with Citrus Vinaigrette and Walnuts 22
Chicken in Coconut Sauce 78
Cooked Olive Salad 24
Meatlovers Meat Sauce 106
Roasted Vegetable Salad 24

Chicken
Chicken Drumsticks Filled with Pickled Lemons, Lentils, and Rice 86
Chicken in Apples, Cinnamon and Caramel Sauce 68
Chicken in Coconut Sauce 78
Chicken in Raisins and Olives 88
Chicken Legs Stuffed with Almonds and Pistachios 90
Chicken Quarters Baked in Parchment Paper 58
Chicken Stew with Israeli Couscous and Vegetables 80
Chicken Stuffed with Ground Meat and Rice 74
Chicken Stuffed with Rice, Mushrooms, and Fresh Herbs 76
Chicken with Artichokes 64
Chicken with Potatoes and Red Peppers 78
Chicken with String Beans 88
Chicken with Sweet Potatoes, Soy Sauce, and Honey 84
Citrus Chicken Thighs 82
Coco: Grandma Ora's Roast Chicken 72
Maschan 60
Paella Chicken 66
Pal'u–Bukharin Rice Dish 70
Sunday Shnitzel 62
Tabchah Balkra'ah: Chicken in Pumpkin and Potatoes 64

Chicken liver
Chicken Livers in Turmeric 52
Chopped Liver 50
Crispy Chicken Liver Salad with Spinach Leaves and Orange Slices 52
Croissants Filled with Chicken Liver 54
Liver with Onion Jam 50
Meatlovers Meat Sauce 106

Coconut
Semolina Cake 131
Yoyo: Fried Biscuits 136

Coconut milk or cream
Asian Chreime on a Bed of Couscous 34
Chicken in Coconut Sauce 78
Coconut Malabi 126

Coriander
Asian Chreime on a Bed of Couscous 34
Braided Puff Pastry with Ground Beef, Eggplant, and Olives 96
Cauliflower, Pepper, and Citrus Casserole 30
Chicken Drumsticks Filled with Pickled Lemons, Lentils, and Rice 86
Chickpea Casserole with Ginger, Tomato, and Date Honey 30
Fresh Herb, Cashew, and Lemon Salad 26
Mafrum Fish in Eggplant, Tomato Sauce and Tahini 46
Meatballs in Lemon Sauce 98
Nile Perch in Tomato, Pepper, Eggplant and Chickpea Sauce 44
Raw Beet Salad 28
Seared Nile Perch in Garlic and Lemon, with Moroccan Salsa 38

Date honey
Cauliflower, Pepper, and Citrus Casserole 30
Chicken Drumsticks Filled with Pickled Lemons, Lentils, and Rice 86
Chickpea Casserole with Ginger, Tomato, and Date Honey 30
Crispy Chicken Liver Salad with Spinach Leaves and Orange Slices 52
Pumpkin in Date Honey and Rosemary 102
Raw Beet Salad 28

Dates
Date Cookies 126

Dough
Baked Apples in Crispy Coating 122
Braided Puff Pastry with Ground Beef, Eggplant, and Olives 96
Cinnamon Buns 124
Date Cookies 126
Halva Squares 134
Puff Pastry Baklava 128
Raybe Biscuits 134
Shabbat Challah 18
Yoyo: Fried Biscuits 136

Dried fruit
Chicken in Raisins and Olives 88
Date Cookies 126
Quinoa and Dried Fruit Salad (dried cranberries or currants) 22
Raw Beet Salad (prunes) 28
Seared Nile Perch in Garlic and Lemon, with Moroccan Salsa (raisins) 38

Eggplant
Braided Puff Pastry with Ground Beef, Eggplant, and Olives 96
Greek Eggplant Salad 24
Mafrum Fish in Eggplant, Tomato Sauce and Tahini 46
Meatballs on a Bed of Eggplant and Tomatoes 104
Meatballs with Eggplant 114
Nile Perch in Tomato, Pepper, Eggplant and Chickpea Sauce 44

Roasted Eggplant and Pepper Salad, with Tahini 26

Eggs
Artichokes Filled with Ground Meat 110
Chopped Liver 50
Crispy Chicken Liver Salad with Spinach Leaves and Orange Slices 52
Daniel's Chocolate Cake 130
Halva Squares 134
Mafrum 118
Meatballs in Artichoke, Fava Bean, and Sage Casserole 112
Meatballs in Lemon Sauce 98
Meatballs on a Bed of Eggplant and Tomatoes 104
Meatballs with Baharat and Hawayij 102
Meatballs with Eggplant 114
Nile Perch with Lemon and Fresh Herbs 40
Semolina Cake 131
Shabbat Challah 18
Sunday Shnitzel 62
Walnut Carrot Cake 132
Yoyo: Fried Biscuits 136

Fava beans
Meatballs in Artichoke, Fava Bean, and Sage Casserole 112
Meatballs with Peas (Fava bean option) 108
White Fava Bean and Olive Oil Spread 91

Fish
Asian Chreime on a Bed of Couscous 34
Mafrum Fish in Eggplant, Tomato Sauce and Tahini 46
Nile Perch in Tomato, Pepper, Eggplant and Chickpea Sauce 44
Nile Perch with Lemon and Fresh Herbs 40
Noodles and Frika with Slices of Fish, Chimichurri, Tomatoes and Pickled Lemons 36
Seared Nile Perch in Garlic and Lemon, with Moroccan Salsa 38
Tuscany Baked Fish 42

Fresh herbs
Chicken Stuffed with Rice, Mushrooms, and Fresh Herbs 76
Fresh Herb, Cashew, and Lemon Salad 26
Nile Perch with Lemon and Fresh Herbs 40
Seared Nile Perch in Garlic and Lemon, with Moroccan Salsa 38
Tuscany Baked Fish 42

Grape leaves
Chicken Quarters Baked in Parchment Paper 58
Grape Leaf Cake, with Meat, Rice, Raisins, and Pistachios 116
Stuffed Onions 94

Green beans
Chicken with String Beans 88

Ground meat
Artichokes Filled with Ground Meat 110
Braided Puff Pastry with Ground Beef, Eggplant, and Olives 96
Chicken Stuffed with Ground Meat and Rice 74
Grape Leaf Cake, with Meat, Rice, Raisins, and Pistachios 116
Mafrum 118
Meatballs in Artichoke, Fava Bean, and Sage Casserole 112
Meatballs in Lemon Sauce 98
Meatballs on a Bed of Eggplant and Tomatoes 104
Meatballs with Baharat and Hawayij 102
Meatballs with Eggplant 114
Meatballs with Peas 108
Meatlovers Meat Sauce 106
Stuffed Onions 94
Tomatoes Stuffed with Ground Meat and Rice 108
Vegetables Stuffed with Meat, Rice, and Lentils 100

Honey
Carrot and Kohlrabi Salad with Citrus Vinaigrette and Walnuts 22
Chicken Stuffed with Rice, Mushrooms, and Fresh Herbs 76
Chicken with Sweet Potatoes, Soy Sauce, and Honey 84
Quinoa and Dried Fruit Salad 22

Hot peppers
Asian Chreime on a Bed of Couscous 34
Beet Tahini with Chickpea and Black Lentil Salad 28
Cauliflower, Pepper, and Citrus Casserole 30
Cherry Tomato Salad with Scallions 25
Chicken in Apples, Cinnamon and Caramel Sauce 68
Chicken Quarters Baked in Parchment Paper 58
Chicken Stuffed with Rice, Mushrooms, and Fresh Herbs 76
Meatballs on a Bed of Eggplant and Tomatoes 104
Nile Perch in Tomato, Pepper, Eggplant and Chickpea Sauce 44
Roasted Eggplant and Pepper Salad, with Tahini 26
Roasted Hot Pepper Salad 25
Roasted Vegetable Salad 24
Swiss Chard Salad 45

Hummus
Beet Tahini with Chickpea and Black Lentil Salad 28
Chickpea Casserole with Ginger, Tomato, and Date Honey 30
Maschan 60
Nile Perch in Tomato, Pepper, Eggplant and Chickpea Sauce 44

Kohlrabi
Carrot and Kohlrabi Salad with Citrus Vinaigrette and Walnuts 22

Leeks
Asian Chreime on a Bed of Couscous 34
Chicken Stew with Israeli Couscous and Vegetables 80

Lemons (pickled also)
Apio: Root Vegetable Dish 29
Beet Tahini with Chickpea and Black Lentil Salad 28
Carrot and Kohlrabi Salad with Citrus Vinaigrette and Walnuts 22
Cauliflower, Pepper, and Citrus Casserole 30
Cherry Tomato Salad with Scallions 25
Chicken Drumsticks Filled with Pickled Lemons, Lentils, and Rice 86
Chicken Quarters Baked in Parchment Paper 58
Chicken Stuffed with Rice, Mushrooms, and Fresh Herbs 76
Chicken with Artichokes 64
Chickpea Casserole with Ginger, Tomato, and Date Honey 30
Citrus Chicken Thighs 82
Cooked Olive Salad 24
Fresh Herb, Cashew, and Lemon Salad 26
Grape Leaf Cake, with Meat, Rice, Raisins, and Pistachios 116
Greek Eggplant Salad 24
Mafrum Fish in Eggplant, Tomato Sauce and Tahini 46
Meatballs in Lemon Sauce 98
Nile Perch with Lemon and Fresh Herbs 40
Puff Pastry Baklava 128
Quince Jam 132
Raw Beet Salad 28
Raybe Biscuits 134
Roasted Eggplant and Pepper Salad, with Tahini 26
Roasted Hot Pepper Salad 25
Roasted Vegetable Salad 24
Seared Nile Perch in Garlic and Lemon, with

Ingredient Index

Moroccan Salsa 38
Swiss Chard Salad 45
Tuscany Baked Fish 42
Yoyo: Fried Biscuits 136

Lentils
Beet Tahini with Chickpea and Black Lentil Salad 28
Chicken Drumsticks Filled with Pickled Lemons, Lentils, and Rice 86
Vegetables Stuffed with Meat, Rice, and Lentils 100

Mint
Beet Tahini with Chickpea and Black Lentil Salad 28
Braided Puff Pastry with Ground Beef, Eggplant, and Olives 96
Chicken Drumsticks Filled with Pickled Lemons, Lentils, and Rice 86
Fresh Herb, Cashew, and Lemon Salad 26
Grape Leaf Cake, with Meat, Rice, Raisins, and Pistachios 116
Mafrum Fish in Eggplant, Tomato Sauce and Tahini 46
Noodles and Frika with Slices of Fish, Chimichurri, Tomatoes and Pickled Lemons 36
Quinoa and Dried Fruit Salad 22
Raw Beet Salad 28
Seared Nile Perch in Garlic and Lemon, with Moroccan Salsa 38
Stuffed Onions 94
Tabchah Balkra'ah: Chicken in Pumpkin and Potatoes 64

Mushrooms
Asian Chreime on a Bed of Couscous 34
Chicken Stuffed with Rice, Mushrooms, and Fresh Herbs 76

Nuts
Baked Apples in Crispy Coating (pistachios, almonds) 122
Braided Puff Pastry with Ground Beef, Eggplant, and Olives (almond flakes) 96
Carrot and Kohlrabi Salad with Citrus Vinaigrette and Walnuts 22
Chicken Legs Stuffed with Almonds and Pistachios (pine nuts) 90
Chicken Stuffed with Ground Meat and Rice (pine nuts) 74
Chicken Stuffed with Rice, Mushrooms, and Fresh Herbs (pine nuts) 76
Crispy Chicken Liver Salad with Spinach Leaves and Orange Slices (pine nuts) 52
Date Cookies (walnuts) 126

Fresh Herb, Cashew, and Lemon Salad 26
Grape Leaf Cake, with Meat, Rice, Raisins, and Pistachios 116
Masapan: Moroccan Marzipan (almonds) 136
Puff Pastry Baklava (peanuts) 128
Quince Jam (walnuts) 132
Raw Beet Salad (pine nuts) 28
Raybe Biscuits (almonds) 134
Semolina Cake (walnuts) 131
Walnut Carrot Cake 132

Olives
Braided Puff Pastry with Ground Beef, Eggplant, and Olives 96
Chicken in Raisins and Olives 88
Cooked Olive Salad 24
Tuscany Baked Fish 42

Onions
Artichokes Filled with Ground Meat 110
Beet Tahini with Chickpea and Black Lentil Salad 28
Braided Puff Pastry with Ground Beef, Eggplant, and Olives 96
Cauliflower, Pepper, and Citrus Casserole 30
Chicken in Coconut Sauce 78
Chicken in Raisins and Olives 88
Chicken Livers in Turmeric 52
Chicken Stuffed with Ground Meat and Rice 74
Chicken Stuffed with Rice, Mushrooms, and Fresh Herbs 76
Chicken with Artichokes 64
Chicken with Potatoes and Red Peppers 78
Chicken with String Beans 88
Chicken with Sweet Potatoes, Soy Sauce, and Honey 84
Chickpea Casserole with Ginger, Tomato, and Date Honey 30
Chopped Liver 50
Coco: Grandma Ora's Roast Chicken 72
Crispy Chicken Liver Salad with Spinach Leaves and Orange Slices 52
Croissants Filled with Chicken Liver 54
Grape Leaf Cake, with Meat, Rice, Raisins, and Pistachios 116
Greek Eggplant Salad 24
Liver with Onion Jam 50
Maschan 60
Meatballs in Artichoke, Fava Bean, and Sage Casserole 112
Meatballs in Lemon Sauce 98
Meatballs with Baharat and Hawayij 102
Meatballs with Peas 108
Meatlovers Meat Sauce 106
Paella Chicken 66
Pal'u–Bukharin Rice Dish 70

Roasted Eggplant and Pepper Salad, with Tahini 26
Roasted Vegetable Salad 24
Stuffed Onions 94
Tabchah Balkra'ah: Chicken in Pumpkin and Potatoes 64
Tomatoes Stuffed with Ground Meat and Rice 108
Vegetables Stuffed with Meat, Rice, and Lentils 100

Oranges
Carrot and Kohlrabi Salad with Citrus Vinaigrette and Walnuts 22
Cauliflower, Pepper, and Citrus Casserole 30
Chicken Stuffed with Rice, Mushrooms, and Fresh Herbs 76
Citrus Chicken Thighs 82
Date Cookies 126
Semolina Cake 131
Yoyo: Fried Biscuits 136

Oregano
Chicken Quarters Baked in Parchment Paper 58
Chicken Stuffed with Rice, Mushrooms, and Fresh Herbs 76
On the Side: White Beans with Fresh Herbs 43
Tuscany Baked Fish 42

Parsley
Artichokes Filled with Ground Meat 110
Beet Tahini with Chickpea and Black Lentil Salad 28
Braided Puff Pastry with Ground Beef, Eggplant, and Olives 96
Carrot and Kohlrabi Salad with Citrus Vinaigrette and Walnuts 22
Cauliflower, Pepper, and Citrus Casserole 30
Chicken Stuffed with Ground Meat and Rice 74
Chicken with Potatoes and Red Peppers 78
Chickpea Casserole with Ginger, Tomato, and Date Honey 30
Fresh Herb, Cashew, and Lemon Salad 26
Grape Leaf Cake, with Meat, Rice, Raisins, and Pistachios 116
Greek Eggplant Salad 24
Meatballs in Artichoke, Fava Bean, and Sage Casserole 112
Meatballs on a Bed of Eggplant and Tomatoes 104
Meatballs with Baharat and Hawayij 102
Meatballs with Peas 108
Meatlovers Meat Sauce 106
Nile Perch with Lemon and Fresh Herbs 40
Noodles and Frika with Slices of Fish, Chimichurri, Tomatoes and Pickled Lemons 36

On the Side: White Beans with Fresh Herbs 43
Roasted Eggplant and Pepper Salad, with Tahini 26
Roasted Vegetable Salad 24
Stuffed Onions 94
Tomatoes Stuffed with Ground Meat and Rice 108
Vegetables Stuffed with Meat, Rice, and Lentils 100

Peas
Meatballs with Peas 108

Peppers
Asian Chreime on a Bed of Couscous 34
Cauliflower, Pepper, and Citrus Casserole 30
Chicken with Potatoes and Red Peppers 78
Greek Eggplant Salad 24
Nile Perch in Tomato, Pepper, Eggplant and Chickpea Sauce 44
Paella Chicken 66
Roasted Eggplant and Pepper Salad, with Tahini 26
Roasted Hot Pepper Salad 25
Roasted Vegetable Salad 24
Seared Nile Perch in Garlic and Lemon, with Moroccan Salsa 38
Vegetables Stuffed with Meat, Rice, and Lentils 100

Pomegranate concentrate
Carrot and Kohlrabi Salad with Citrus Vinaigrette and Walnuts 22
Cherry Tomato Salad with Scallions 25
Quinoa and Dried Fruit Salad 22
Raw Beet Salad 28

Potatoes
Chicken in Apples, Cinnamon and Caramel Sauce 68
Chicken Stew with Israeli Couscous and Vegetables 80
Chicken with Potatoes and Red Peppers 78
Coco: Grandma Ora's Roast Chicken 72
Mafrum 118
Meatlovers Meat Sauce 106
Stuffed Onions 94
Tabchah Balkra'ah: Chicken in Pumpkin and Potatoes 64

Pumpkin
Pumpkin in Date Honey and Rosemary 102
Tabchah Balkra'ah: Chicken in Pumpkin and Potatoes 64
Walnut Carrot Cake (pumpkin option) 132

Rice
Chicken Drumsticks Filled with Pickled Lemons, Lentils, and Rice 86
Chicken Stuffed with Ground Meat and Rice 74
Chicken Stuffed with Rice, Mushrooms, and Fresh Herbs 76
Grape Leaf Cake, with Meat, Rice, Raisins, and Pistachios 116
Maschan 60
Paella Chicken 66
Pal'u–Bukharin Rice Dish 70
Steamed Basmati Rice 31
Tomatoes Stuffed with Ground Meat and Rice 108
Vegetables Stuffed with Meat, Rice, and Lentils 100

Rosemary
Chicken Drumsticks Filled with Pickled Lemons, Lentils, and Rice 86
Chicken Quarters Baked in Parchment Paper 58
Chicken Stuffed with Rice, Mushrooms, and Fresh Herbs 76
Nile Perch with Lemon and Fresh Herbs 40
Pumpkin in Date Honey and Rosemary 102

Salads
Beet Tahini with Chickpea and Black Lentil Salad 28
Carrot and Kohlrabi Salad with Citrus Vinaigrette and Walnuts 22
Cherry Tomato Salad with Scallions 25
Cooked Olive Salad 24
Fresh Herb, Cashew, and Lemon Salad 26
Greek Eggplant Salad 24
Raw Beet Salad 28
Roasted Eggplant and Pepper Salad, with Tahini 26
Roasted Hot Pepper Salad 25

Scallions (green onions)
Cauliflower, Pepper, and Citrus Casserole 30
Cherry Tomato Salad with Scallions 25
Liver with Onion Jam 50
Meatlovers Meat Sauce 106
Paella Chicken 66

Semolina
Semolina Cake 131

Sweet potatoes
Chicken in Apples, Cinnamon and Caramel Sauce 68
Chicken with Sweet Potatoes, Soy Sauce, and Honey 84

Swiss chard
Meatballs in Lemon Sauce 98
Swiss Chard Salad 45

Tahini or Halva
Beet Tahini with Chickpea and Black Lentil Salad 28
Halva Squares 134
Mafrum Fish in Eggplant, Tomato Sauce and Tahini 46
Roasted Eggplant and Pepper Salad, with Tahini 26

Thyme
Chicken Drumsticks Filled with Pickled Lemons, Lentils, and Rice 86
Chicken Stuffed with Rice, Mushrooms, and Fresh Herbs 76
Citrus Chicken Thighs 82
Croissants Filled with Chicken Liver 54
Liver with Onion Jam 50
Nile Perch with Lemon and Fresh Herbs 40
On the Side: White Beans with Fresh Herbs 43

Tomatoes and cherry tomatoes
Asian Chreime on a Bed of Couscous 34
Cauliflower, Pepper, and Citrus Casserole 30
Cherry Tomato Salad with Scallions 25
Chicken Stuffed with Ground Meat and Rice 74
Chickpea Casserole with Ginger, Tomato, and Date Honey 30
Cooked Olive Salad 24
Mafrum 118
Mafrum Fish in Eggplant, Tomato Sauce and Tahini 46
Meatballs in Artichoke, Fava Bean, and Sage Casserole 112
Meatballs on a Bed of Eggplant and Tomatoes 104
Meatballs with Baharat and Hawayij 102
Nile Perch in Tomato, Pepper, Eggplant and Chickpea Sauce 44
Noodles and Frika with Slices of Fish, Chimichurri, Tomatoes and Pickled Lemons 36
Paella Chicken 66
Roasted Vegetable Salad 24
Tabchah Balkra'ah: Chicken in Pumpkin and Potatoes 64
Tomatoes Stuffed with Ground Meat and Rice 108
Tuscany Baked Fish 42
Vegetables Stuffed with Meat, Rice, and Lentils 100

White beans
On the Side: White Beans with Fresh Herbs 43

Story Index

All of the stories and fables are based on folktales

Bank of Time 71
Be Yourself 97
Butterfly, The 37
Child of Shabbat 19
Clock, The 87
Cookie Bag, The 125
Coping with Problems 41
Cracked Bucket, The 91
Criticism and Dirty Laundry 31
Experience 127
Experiment, The 131
Farm, The 117
Fisherman, The 45
Frog's Tale, The 109
G-d's Coffee 129
Glass of Milk, A 135
Golden Cage, The 83
Harvard and Stanford 113
I Ate Lunch With G-d 111
Invitation 101
Island, The 69
King Who Had Four Wives, The 76
Large Stones of Life, The 84
Lesson in Modesty, A 122
Life 75
Listen to a Whisper or Wait for a Rude Awakening 27
Love Box, The 137
Man and the Monkey, The 63
Mend the World 25
More Precious Than Diamonds 105
Mountain, The 39
No Price for Love 79
On The Quality of Hearing 103
Only a Smile 115
Our True Worth 119
Painting, The 61
Pair of Socks, A 43
Path of Life 106
Policy of Monkeys, The 81
Power of Cooperation, The 53
Put Down the Glass Today 99
Remembering the Good; Forgetting the Bad 29
Respect 65
Scottish Farmer and Penicillin, The 67

Story of Love, The 51
Story of the Nails in the Fence, The 47
Stranger Came to Stay, A 94
Tale of Two Brothers, A 35
Tale of Two Monks, A 55
Thank you 59
Tools from Hashem, The 72
Tree, The 89
Wheel Goes Round, The 23
Wine Vinegar 133

142

Photographer and Stylist Index

Photographers

Ilit Azolay
13, 27 (right side, upper and lower), 40, 41 (left), 42 (right), 47, 73, 74 (right), 79, 91, 96, 97, 192, 103, 105 (right), 109, 114 (right), 115, 126 (right)

Shachar Fleischmann
42 (left), 43, 50 (right), 68, 69, 77, 87, 132 (middle and left), 133

Kfir Harbi
65, 95, 104, 105 (middle), 107

Eran Lam
9, 101, 89

Gilad Larom
28 (left), 36, 38 (right), 52, 59, 62, 74 (left), 98 (trio on left), 99, 108, 114 (left), 121, 124, 125

Daniel Layla
22, 23 (right), 58, 61 (left), 90, 126 (left), 127, 128, 129, 136 (right and middle)

Michal Lenart
11, 20 (left), 29, 37, 53, 60, 61 (right), 70, 80, 81, 116, 117

Philip Metrai
46, 86 (left)

Yossi Salis
20 (right), 21, 23 (middle and left), 24, 25, 26, 32 (right), 33 (left), 34, 35, 41 (right), 44, 45, 48, 49, 50 (left), 57, 78 (left), 82, 83, 98 (right), 100, 112, 113, 134 (left)

Adi Shiovits and photographic assistant Doron Gafni
16, 17, 136 (left)

Danya Weiner
30, 31, 39, 56, 66, 67, 72, 75, 85, 122, 123

Danny Yanai
63

Yasmin & Arye Photographers
7, 32 (left), 38 (left and middle), 51, 54, 64, 71, 78 (right), 84, 86 (right), 88, 92, 93, 105 (left), 110, 118, 119, 120, 130, 131 (right), 134 (right), 135, 137

Stylists

Chanoch Bar Shalom
46, 86, 58 (left), 90

Natasha Haimovich
20 (right), 21, 24, 25, 26, 33 (left), 34, 35, 41 (right), 44, 45, 48, 49, 50 (left), 57, 82, 83, 98 (right), 100, 112, 113, 134 (left)

Dariya Karagula
42 (left), 43, 68, 69, 77, 87, 132 (middle and left), 133

Nurit Kariv
28 (left), 36, 38, 52, 54, 62, 64, 74 (left), 78 (right), 84, 88, 92, 93, 98 (trio on left), 108, 110, 114 (left), 118, 119 (right) 125, 132 (right), 134 (right), 135

ShantiHouse
A Warm Home for Youth At Risk

WARM HOMES FOR AT-RISK YOUTH

SHANTI HOUSE SUPPORTERS GROUP

A CHANCE TO SAVE 2,500 CHILDREN A YEAR!

The residents at Shanti House are young people who were forced to leave their homes and, finding themselves homeless, were otherwise in imminent danger of physical violence, sexual abuse, delinquency, prostitution and more.

For many of them, this is the last chance for a warm and loving home before descending to life on the streets.

During its 31 years of operation, Shanti House has survived thanks mainly to donations, enabling it to help tens of thousands of young people in Israel.

We invite you to join a group of supporters who donate a minimum of USD 8.25 per month, thereby creating a human safety net.

Together we will ensure that every year thousands of young people will have a warm home and a supportive family.

JOIN AS A SUPPORTER OF SHANTI HOUSE

Visit the website, sign the petition
And we will contact you by phone

www.shanti.org.il

Thank you,

The Children of Shanti House

---

17 Simtat Shlush, P.O. Box 50041, Tel Aviv 6150001, ISRAEL.
Tel. 972-3-5103339, Fax. 972-3-5168603